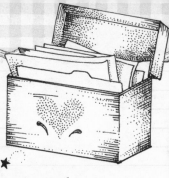

YOUR recipe could appear in our next cookbook!

Share your tried & true family favorites with us instantly at

www.gooseberrypatch.com

If you'd rather jot 'em down by hand, just mail this form to...

Gooseberry Patch • Cookbooks – Call for Recipes
PO Box 812 • Columbus, OH 43216-0812

If your recipe is selected for a book, you'll receive a FREE copy!

Please share only your original recipes or those that you have made your own over the years.

Recipe Name:

Number of Servings:

Any fond memories about this recipe? Special touches you like to add or handy shortcuts?

Ingredients (include specific measurements):

S0-BRI-519

Instructions (continue on back if needed):

Special Code: **cookbookspage**

Over ➤

Extra space for recipe if needed:

Tell us about yourself...

Your complete contact information is needed so that we can send you your FREE cookbook, if your recipe is published. Phone numbers and email addresses are kept private and will only be used if we have questions about your recipe.

Name:

Address:

City: State: Zip:

Email:

Daytime Phone:

Thank you! Vickie & Jo Ann

GRILLING AND CAMPFIRE COOKING

Gooseberry Patch

An imprint of Globe Pequot
246 Goose Lane
Guilford, CT 06437

www.gooseberrypatch.com

1•800•854•6673

Copyright 2021, Gooseberry Patch 978-1-62093-419-7

Photo Edition is a major revision of *Grillling and Campfire Cooking.*

Do you have a tried & true recipe...

tip, craft or memory that you'd like to see featured in
a **Gooseberry Patch** cookbook? Visit our website at
www.gooseberrypatch.com and follow the
easy steps to submit your favorite family recipe.
Or send them to us at:

Gooseberry Patch
PO Box 812
Columbus, OH 43216-0812

Don't forget to include the number of servings your recipe makes,
plus your name, address, phone number and email address. If we
select your recipe, your name will appear right along with it...
and you'll receive a **FREE** copy of the book!

CONTENTS

DEDICATION

To everyone who loves backyard burgers, toasted marshmallows and picnics with friends...and knows that eating outdoors just makes everything taste better!

APPRECIATION

A big thanks to all of you who shared your most delicious grilling and camping recipes with us.

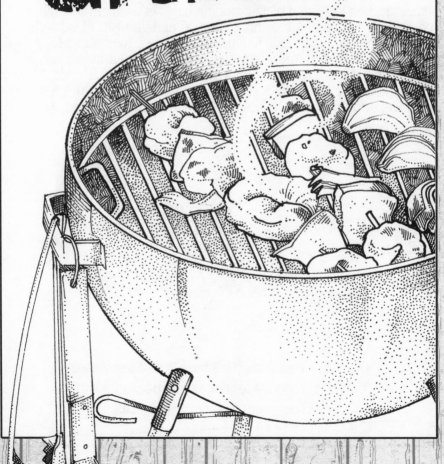

Rich's Charcoal Lemon-Lime Chicken

Kelly Greene
Riverside, CA

This recipe is my stepdad's. It is always requested when we go to visit him...terrific for tailgating!

6 boneless, skinless chicken
  breasts
1/2 c. brown sugar, packed
1/4 c. cider vinegar
3 T. coarse mustard
juice of 1 lime
juice of 1/2 lemon

3 cloves garlic, pressed
1-1/2 t. salt, or to taste
pepper to taste
6 T. oil
Garnish: lemon slices, chopped
  fresh herbs

Place chicken in a large plastic zipping bag; set aside. In a bowl, combine remaining ingredients except oil and garnish. Blend well; whisk in oil. Add marinade to chicken; seal bag. Refrigerate for 8 hours to overnight, turning occasionally. One hour before serving time, bring chicken to room temperature, discarding marinade. Place chicken on an oiled grate over medium-high heat. Grill for 4 minutes per side, or until chicken juices run clear. Garnish as desired. Serves 6.

Using jute, bundle together fresh herbs like rosemary,
thyme or marjoram to create an herb basting brush...
it really adds flavor to grilled foods.

HOT OFF THE GRILL

Tangy Peach-Glazed Chicken

Kathleen Sturm
Corona, CA

*I made this delicious grilled chicken for my sister many years ago.
She just had to have the recipe that night! Now she makes it
for her family often.*

3 lbs. chicken
1 c. peach jam or preserves
2 T. oil
1 T. plus 1 t. soy sauce
1 T. dry mustard

1 clove garlic, minced
1/4 t. cayenne pepper
1 t. salt
1/2 t. pepper

Place chicken on an oiled grate over medium-high heat. Grill for 30 to
40 minutes. Meanwhile, combine remaining ingredients in a bowl;
mix well. Brush peach mixture generously over chicken during last
10 minutes of cooking. Grill until chicken juices run clear when
pierced. Makes 8 servings.

Sweet & Spicy Chicken

Kristin Pittis
Dennison, OH

*This chicken is delicious! Serve with a baked potato and
steamed fresh green beans for a dinner you'll love.*

1/2 c. light brown sugar, packed
2 T. chili powder
1 t. seasoned salt

1/2 t. garlic powder
4 boneless, skinless chicken
breasts

In a large plastic zipping bag, combine all ingredients except chicken.
Pat chicken dry; add to bag. Seal bag and rub brown sugar mixture
into chicken. Refrigerate for at least 30 minutes. Place chicken on an
oiled grate over medium-high heat. Grill for 8 to 10 minutes on each
side, until chicken juices run clear. Makes 4 servings.

April's Barbecue Chicken

April Kofler
Santa Cruz, CA

My uncle was a chef. He shared this recipe with me 30 years ago, and I have changed it a little. This is the only BBQ chicken recipe I use, and I use this delicious sauce on everything from ribs to pulled pork. I like my sauce sweet, so I just taste as it cooks to see if I need to add more brown sugar to the sauce.

3 lbs. chicken, or 6 chicken
   breasts
1 T. plus 1 t. garlic powder,
   divided
1-1/2 t. onion powder, divided
2 c. catsup

1 to 2 c. brown sugar, packed
   and divided
1/2 t. dry mustard
1/2 t. chili powder
1 t. smoke-flavored cooking
   sauce

Place chicken in a large stockpot over medium-high heat. Cover with water; add one tablespoon garlic powder and one teaspoon onion powder. Bring to a boil. Reduce heat; cover and cook for about 15 minutes. Meanwhile, in a saucepan over medium heat, mix together catsup, one cup brown sugar, mustard, chili powder and remaining garlic and onion powders. Add remaining brown sugar to taste. Simmer about 15 minutes; add cooking sauce and cook another few minutes. Place chicken on an oiled grate over medium-high heat. Grill for 30 to 40 minutes, turning and basting often with sauce, until chicken juices run clear. Makes 6 to 8 servings.

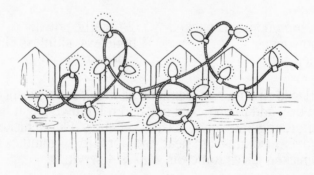

Wind twinkling yellow or white lights along the garden fence
and in the trees for a twinkling firefly effect as the sun sets.

HOT OFF THE GRILL

Bacon-Wrapped BBQ Chicken

Nicole Culver
La Fontaine, IN

Over the 4th of July, my sister-in-law Kim cooked this chicken for us on her tiny grill, and I fell in love! Since then, my husband has added his own touch to it. Serve with corn on the cob, watermelon and a cold glass of iced tea for a sunny summer dinner.

18-oz. bottle favorite barbecue
   sauce, divided
2 T. brown sugar, packed
onion powder to taste

4 to 6 boneless, skinless chicken
   breasts
1/2 to 1 lb. bacon

In a saucepan over low heat, combine sauce, brown sugar and onion powder. Simmer for 30 minutes, stirring occasionally. Meanwhile, wrap chicken breasts with one to 2 slices bacon each; secure with wooden toothpicks. Set aside 3/4 cup of sauce mixture. Brush remaining sauce mixture over chicken. Place chicken on an oiled grate over medium-high heat. Grill for 30 minutes, turning occasionally, until nearly done. Brush chicken well with reserved sauce mixture. Cook until chicken juices run clear and sauce is caramelized. Serves 4 to 6.

Pesto-Brie Grilled Chicken

Brenda Schlosser
Brighton, CO

A dish I came up with just for the love of basil and brie together. Serve with angel hair pasta tossed with olive oil, sun-dried tomatoes and fresh garlic...wonderful!

4 boneless, skinless chicken
   breasts
1/4 c. basil pesto sauce

4 slices brie cheese, 1/4-inch
   thick
salt and pepper to taste

Place chicken on an oiled grate over medium-high heat. Grill for 3 to 5 minutes; turn chicken over. Spread each piece with one tablespoon pesto and top with a cheese slice. Cover; continue cooking for 3 to 5 minutes, until cheese is melted and chicken juices run clear. Serves 4.

Kansas City Pork Chops

Krista Marshall
Fort Wayne, IN

*These grilled pork chops will make your backyard smell like a smokin'
barbecue joint. They are bursting with flavor and so easy!*

4 thin center-cut pork loin chops
1/4 c. brown sugar, packed
2 T. paprika
1-1/2 t. garlic powder
1-1/2 t. chili powder

1-1/2 t. onion powder
1-1/2 t. salt
1-1/2 t. pepper
favorite barbecue sauce to taste

Place pork chops in a plastic zipping bag; set aside. Mix together brown
sugar and seasonings in a small bowl. Add mixture to bag. Close bag
tightly and shake to coat pork chops. Refrigerate at least 2 hours.
Place pork chops on an oiled grate over medium-high heat. Grill for
3 minutes on each side. Reduce heat to low. Continue cooking for
about 7 minutes on each side, until pork juices run clear. During the
last 2 minutes on each side, baste with barbecue sauce. Remove from
heat; baste with a little extra sauce before serving. Makes 4 servings.

Trim excess fat from meat before it's grilled to cut down on flare-ups.
A squirt bottle of water is handy for putting out flames.

Grilled Ham & Pineapple

Sharon Dennison
Floyds Knobs, IN

A delicious combination! Grilled fresh pineapple can't be beat,
but if time is short, use canned pineapple slices, adding them
to the grill when the ham is almost done.

1 fresh pineapple
3 T. honey
1/4 c. mustard
1/4 c. pineapple juice
2 T. brown sugar, packed

1/2 t. prepared horseradish
1/8 t. salt
1-1/2 to 2-lb. ham steak,
  1-inch thick

Remove top of pineapple but do not peel. Cut lengthwise into
8 wedges. Place wedges in a pan and brush with honey. Cover and
refrigerate for one hour, turning occasionally. Place pineapple wedges
skin-side down on an oiled grate over medium-high heat. Grill for
20 minutes, or until hot. Meanwhile, for sauce, mix together remaining
ingredients except ham. Cut ham steak into serving-size pieces, if
desired. Grill ham, brushing often with sauce, until glazed and heated
through. Serve ham with pineapple and remaining sauce for drizzling.
Serves 4 to 6.

Old-fashioned Mason jars make lovely lanterns for backyard gatherings!
Nestle a tea light inside and hang with wire from tree branches or
fenceposts. Look for citronella candles to keep mosquitoes away.

Tom's BBQ Ribs

Ashley Compoli
Delhi, Ontario

My husband Tom is the BBQ chef at our house. He always fixes ribs this way, and they are wonderful!

2 T. chili powder
1 T. paprika
1 T. garlic salt
1 T. pepper

1 t. cayenne pepper
5 lbs. pork back ribs
brown sugar barbecue sauce to taste

Combine all spices in a small bowl. Coat ribs with spice mixture on both sides; wrap ribs in a double thickness of aluminum foil. Bake at 350 degrees for about 20 minutes. Preheat grill on high; remove ribs from oven and turn grill down to medium. Place ribs, still wrapped in foil, on grate. Cook for about one hour, turning occasionally, until tender. Remove ribs from grill. Increase grill to high heat; brush grill lightly with oil. Unwrap ribs and place on grate; brush with barbecue sauce. Cover and grill for about 5 minutes per side, brushing again with barbecue sauce, until slightly blackened. Cut into serving-size pieces. Makes 4 to 6 servings.

The true essentials of a feast are only food and fun.
– Oliver Wendell Holmes, Sr.

Lazy-Day Grilled Ribs

Penny Sherman
Ava, MO

*Pop these spicy ribs in the oven for the afternoon, then grill briefly
before dinnertime...what could be simpler for a weekend meal?*

2-1/2 T. coarse salt
1-1/2 T. light brown sugar,
   packed
1-1/2 T. chili powder
3/4 t. coarse pepper

4 to 4-1/2 lbs. pork spareribs,
   cut into serving-size pieces
1 c. tangy barbecue sauce,
   divided

In a small bowl, mix together salt, brown sugar and spices. Rub salt
mixture evenly over both sides of ribs. Transfer ribs, bone-side down,
and slightly overlapping, to a rimmed baking sheet. Cover tightly with
aluminum foil. Bake at 300 degrees for 2-1/2 to 3 hours, until tender.
Unwrap ribs and place on an oiled grate over medium-high heat.
Cook for 2 to 5 minutes per side, brushing with 1/2 cup barbecue
sauce, until slightly blackened. Serve remaining sauce alongside ribs.
Serves 4 to 6.

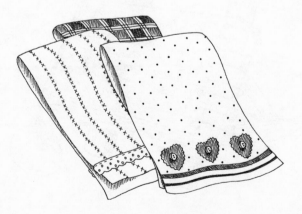

Vintage tea towels make whimsical oversized napkins...so handy for messy-
but-tasty foods like barbecued ribs, buttered corn on the cob
and juicy wedges of watermelon!

Spicy Rubbed Pork Tenderloin

Lynn Rusk
South Bend, IN

This recipe was given to me by my mother-in-law Lynette.
It's a great go-to recipe for company or a busy day at home.

1 to 3 T. chili powder, to taste
1 t. salt
1 t. pepper
1/4 t. ground ginger

1/4 t. dried thyme
1/4 t. dry mustard
1-lb. pork tenderloin fillet

Mix together all spices in a bowl. Rub desired amount of spice mixture over both sides of tenderloin. Wrap tightly in aluminum foil; refrigerate for 8 hours to overnight. Unwrap tenderloin and place on an oiled grate over medium-high heat. Grill to desired doneness, turning once or twice, about 15 to 20 minutes. Remove tenderloin to a platter; let stand for 10 minutes. Slice thinly and serve with natural juices. Makes 8 servings.

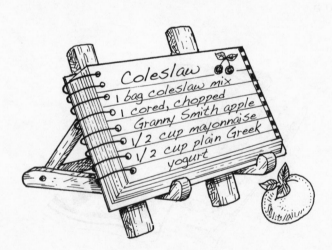

Coleslaw
1 bag coleslaw mix
1 cored, chopped
Granny Smith apple
1/2 cup mayonnaise
1/2 cup plain Greek
yogurt

Here's a tasty apple coleslaw that goes well with pork. Simply toss together a large bag of coleslaw mix, a cored and chopped Granny Smith apple, 1/2 cup of mayonnaise and 1/2 cup plain Greek yogurt.

HOT OFF THE GRILL

Evelyn's Grilled Pork Loin

Diane Brulc
Brookfield, WI

My mom made this for our family get-togethers to serve with all our favorite sides. We always played a game outdoors before dinner. Such fond memories!

3-lb. boneless pork loin roast
1 c. soy sauce
1/2 c. sherry or apple juice
1 t. mustard
1 t. ground ginger
1/2 t. salt
1/4 t. garlic powder

Place roast in a shallow glass dish. Combine remaining ingredients in a bowl and pour over roast. Cover and refrigerate for 2 hours to overnight. Drain marinade into a small saucepan; bring to a boil for 3 minutes. Place roast on a grate over medium-high heat, 6 to 8 inches above heat. Grill, covered, for 1-1/2 to 2 hours, turning and brushing with marinade every 30 minutes. Slice roast thinly to serve. Serves 6 to 8.

Polynesian Ginger Spareribs

Jill Valentine
Jackson, TN

Slice the grilled spareribs into single ribs for a yummy appetizer.

1/2 c. soy sauce
1/2 c. brown sugar, packed
1/2 c. green onions, chopped
1/4 c. catsup
2 cloves garlic, pressed
1 t. fresh ginger, peeled and grated
3 lbs. pork spareribs, cut into serving-size portions

In a microwave-safe dish, mix all ingredients except spareribs. Add spareribs; turn until well coated. Drain marinade into a bowl. Cover ribs with plastic wrap; let stand for 10 minutes. Microwave ribs on medium-high setting for 12 to 16 minutes. Bring marinade to a boil for 3 minutes. Place ribs on an oiled grate over medium-high heat; brush with marinade. Grill for 8 to 10 minutes, turning and brushing once or twice with marinade. Serves 4 to 6.

Savory Flat-Iron Steak

Diana Chaney
Olathe, KS

This newer cut of beef is flavorful and budget-friendly...
I'm glad I gave it a try!

1-1/2 lbs. beef flat-iron steak
   or top blade steak
1/4 c. olive oil
2 T. balsamic vinegar

2 cloves garlic, pressed
1 t. Italian seasoning
salt and pepper to taste

Place steak in a large plastic zipping bag; set aside. Whisk together remaining ingredients in a small bowl; pour over steak. Close bag; refrigerate for one to 8 hours, turning occasionally. Drain, discarding marinade. Place steak on an oiled grate over medium-high heat; grill for 5 minutes. Turn steak over; move to a slightly cooler part of grill. Grill about 4 minutes, to medium-rare or medium. Remove steak to a serving platter; let stand for several minutes. To serve, thinly slice steak across the grain. Serves 6.

Safety first! Be sure to place grilled meat on a clean plate,
never on a plate that previously held raw meat.

Triple Garlic Steak Sandwiches

Alicia Van Duyne
Braidwood, IL

My husband and I both love garlic. We came up with this recipe one evening when we were experimenting with the grill. My children love these sandwiches, and I've had many requests to make them!

1 lb. sliced mushrooms
1 onion, thinly sliced
1 green pepper, thinly sliced
2 t. extra-virgin olive oil
2 t. garlic powder
6 thin-cut boneless beef ribeye
    steaks or sliced beef
    sandwich steaks

2 t. garlic salt
6 slices mozzarella cheese
1/2 c. butter, softened
3 T. garlic, pressed
6 hard rolls, split
Optional: favorite steak sauce

Place vegetables on a long piece of heavy-duty aluminum foil. Sprinkle with olive oil and garlic powder. Place foil on grate over medium-high heat. Grill until vegetables are tender, about 10 to 12 minutes; remove from grill and set aside. Add steaks to grill and sprinkle with garlic salt. Cook to desired doneness, about 2 to 3 minutes per side. Remove from grill; top with cheese slices and keep warm. Blend butter and pressed garlic in a small bowl. Spread butter mixture over cut sides of rolls. Grill rolls cut-side down until toasted. To serve, top each roll with a steak, a spoonful of vegetable mixture and some steak sauce, if desired. Serves 6.

Turn your favorite sliced or shredded pork, beef or chicken barbecue into party food. Serve up bite-size sliders using brown & serve rolls as mini buns.

Grilled London Broil

Liz Lanza
Brownsville, PA

My family has been enjoying this luscious steak for years.
It's so easy to prepare, and the simple marinade is delicious.

3 to 4-lb. beef flank steak   1/3 c. soy sauce
2/3 c. teriyaki sauce

Place steak in a glass casserole dish. Mix together sauces in a small bowl; pour over steak. Cover and refrigerate 8 hours to overnight, turning occasionally. Drain, discarding marinade. Grill steak over high heat to desired doneness, about 4 to 5 minutes on each side for medium. Remove steak from grill; let stand for 10 minutes. Slice steak thinly across the grain. Serves 8 to 10.

Asian Flank Steak

Nancy Girard
Chesapeake, VA

I've been using this recipe for quite awhile, and we really like the
flavor. When I served it at a party, I received rave reviews.

2 to 3-lb. beef flank steak   2 to 3 green onions, thinly sliced
3/4 c. soy sauce   2 cloves garlic, minced
1/4 c. sesame oil   2 t. sugar
2 T. sake or white vinegar

Lightly score steak diagonally on both sides; set aside. Combine remaining ingredients in a shallow glass dish. Add steak; turn to coat. Cover and refrigerate up to 8 hours. Drain, discarding marinade. Grill steak over medium-high heat to desired doneness, about 10 minutes per side, reducing heat to medium if cooking too fast. Let steak stand for 10 minutes. Slice thinly across the grain. Serves 6 to 8.

An instant-read digital thermometer is so handy for checking doneness...no guesswork needed. See page 217 for our handy temperature chart.

Gwen's Pit Beef

Gwen Stutler
Emporia, KS

I love this beef...it's hard to resist nibbling on it straight from the cutting board! It's perfect for hot days because you don't have to heat up the house.

1 T. dried oregano	1 T. salt
1 T. dried thyme	1 T. pepper
1 T. garlic powder	3 to 4-lb. beef top round or
1 T. lemon pepper	eye round roast

Combine spices in a small bowl. Pierce roast all over with a fork; rub and pat spice mixture all over roast. Preheat grill to highest setting. Place roast on an oiled grate. Cover and cook for about 25 to 35 minutes, turning every 7 minutes, until blackened on all sides. Use a meat thermometer inserted into center of roast, 140 degrees for rare, 145 degrees for medium-rare, 160 degrees for medium or 170 degrees for well-done. Remove from heat; let stand for 10 minutes. Slice thinly. Makes 6 to 8 servings.

Nothing beats the taste of fresh-picked herbs and vegetables! Even the smallest yard is sure to have a sunny corner where you can grow sun-ripened tomatoes and an herb or two in a wooden half-barrel. Seeds, plants and free advice are available at the nearest garden store.

Zesty Beef Fajitas

Tomi Russell
Algonquin, IL

My favorite marinated beef for fajitas! This marinade may be refrigerated in an airtight container for up to two days.

2 lbs. beef skirt steak
2 c. pineapple juice
1/4 c. lime juice
1 c. soy sauce
2 T. ground cumin
1-1/2 t. garlic, minced
2 to 3 T. olive oil
1 to 2 red and/or green peppers, thinly sliced
1 onion, thinly sliced
1/2 lb. sliced mushrooms
4 to 6 8-inch flour tortillas, warmed
Garnish: shredded lettuce, chopped tomatoes, shredded Cheddar or Monterey Jack cheese, sour cream, guacamole

Place steak in a plastic zipping bag; set aside. Combine juices, soy sauce, cumin and garlic in a bowl. Whisk, making sure to break up any lumps. Pour marinade over steak; seal bag. Refrigerate for 6 to 8 hours, turning occasionally. Drain and discard marinade. Place steak on an oiled grate over medium-high heat. Grill to desired doneness, about 3 to 4 minutes per side. Meanwhile, heat olive oil in a skillet over medium heat. Sauté vegetables until tender; drain. Top warmed tortillas with sliced steak, vegetables and desired toppings. Makes 4 to 6 servings.

A ridged cast-iron grill skillet is oh-so handy for grilling on your stovetop whenever it's too cold or rainy to use the grill outdoors.

Mustard & Herb Strip Steak

Dale Duncan
Waterloo, IA

A delicious special-occasion recipe! Sometimes I'll serve the sliced steak over polenta or even a big garden salad.

2 to 3 cloves garlic, pressed
2 t. water
2 T. Dijon mustard
1 t. dried basil
1/2 t. dried thyme

1/2 t. pepper
2 8-oz. beef strip steaks or
    top loin steaks, 3/4" thick
salt to taste

Combine garlic and water in a microwave-safe glass measuring cup. Microwave on high setting for 30 seconds. Stir in mustard, herbs and pepper. Brush mixture over both sides of steaks. Place steaks on an oiled grate over medium heat. Cover and grill to desired doneness, 11 minutes for medium-rare or 14 minutes for medium, turning occasionally. Season steaks with salt, as desired. Slice steaks crosswise into thick slices. Serves 2 to 4.

Hankering for steaks on the grill, but finding T-bones and ribeyes too expensive? Try flank or skirt steak. Both are budget-priced yet tender and flavorful when marinated well and sliced thinly. Newer cuts like flat-iron steak are delicious too. Ask your butcher for some friendly tips!

Garlic & Cilantro Chicken

Edie DeSpain
Logan, UT

Marinading the chicken for a full six hours will give you the best flavor. Not a fan of cilantro? Substitute parsley instead.

6 chicken breasts or 8 chicken
    thighs
1 c. low-sodium chicken broth
2 T. olive oil

1 T. fresh cilantro, chopped
6 to 8 cloves garlic, pressed
1/2 t. salt
1 t. coarse pepper

Place chicken in a large plastic zipping bag; set aside. Combine remaining ingredients in a bowl; mix well and pour over chicken. Seal bag; turn to coat chicken with marinade. Refrigerate for 30 minutes to 6 hours, turning bag occasionally. Drain marinade into a small saucepan; bring to a boil for 3 minutes. Place chicken on an oiled grate over medium-high heat. Grill for 30 to 40 minutes, turning twice and brushing with marinade, until chicken juices run clear. Makes 6 to 8 servings.

Gas or charcoal? Every cookout chef has his or her own opinion!
A good rule of thumb is charcoal for taste, gas for haste.

Ginger-Lime Grilled Salmon

Vickie
Gooseberry Patch

A tropical treat, made zesty with fresh grated ginger
and freshly squeezed lime juice.

2 T. butter, melted
2 T. fresh ginger, peeled and
    minced
2 T. lime zest
1 T. lime juice

1/2 t. salt
1/2 t. pepper
2 lbs. salmon fillets, 1-inch thick
Garnish: lime wedges

In a small bowl, combine all ingredients except salmon and garnish.
Rub mixture over salmon fillets. Place fish on a lightly oiled grate over
medium-high heat. Cover and grill about 5 minutes on each side, until
fish flakes easily with a fork. Garnish with lime wedges. Serves 4 to 6.

Cedar Plank Salmon

Jessica Kraus
Delaware, OH

A fantastic smoky salmon...the topping will make
your guests say, "Yum, what is that?" Serve with
roasted veggies and rice.

1 cedar grilling plank
2 12-oz. salmon fillets
salt and pepper to taste

2 t. Dijon mustard
2 t. brown sugar, packed

In a glass dish, cover cedar plank with salted water. Soak for 1-1/2 to
2 hours; drain. Season salmon with salt and pepper; spread evenly
with mustard and sprinkle with brown sugar. Heat grill to medium or
medium-high. Place plank on a grate over indirect heat; preheat for
about 5 minutes. Place fish on plank; cover and cook until fish flakes
easily with a fork, about 20 to 30 minutes. Serves 2 to 4.

Haddock & Creamy Dill Sauce

Claudia Keller
Carrollton, GA

We've been trying to eat more fish lately, so I was happy to find this recipe. It's perfect with tiny new potatoes and grilled asparagus.

1 lb. haddock fillets
1 T. olive oil
salt and pepper to taste
1/2 c. sour cream

1 T. fresh dill, chopped
1 t. lemon juice
Garnish: fresh dill sprigs, thinly
    sliced lemon

Brush fish with oil; season with salt and pepper. Place on a lightly oiled grate over medium heat. Grill for about 4 minutes on each side, turning once, until fish flakes easily with a fork. Stir together remaining ingredients except garnish. Serve fillets topped with sauce; garnish as desired. Serves 4.

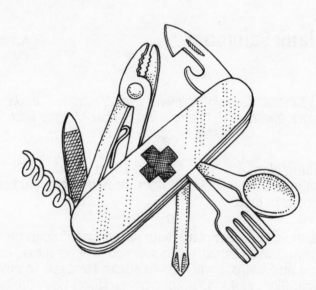

Keep a scout-style pocketknife with can opener, corkscrew and other tools in your cookout kit...you'll wonder what you ever did without it!

Grilled Halibut & Lemon Sauce

Dia Cornell
Vallejo, CA

This is a quick and delicious, fresh-tasting fish and sauce that always impresses.

1/4 c. dry white wine or
   chicken broth
3 T. lemon juice
1 t. dried oregano

1/2 t. salt
1/8 t. pepper
2 lbs. halibut steak, 1-inch thick

Place all ingredients except fish into a large plastic zipping bag; mix well. Add fish to bag; seal and refrigerate for 30 minutes to 2 hours. Drain marinade into a small saucepan; bring to a boil for 3 minutes. Place fish on a lightly oiled grate over medium heat. Grill for 10 to 12 minutes, turning once and brushing with reserved marinade, until fish flakes easily with a fork. Serve with Lemon Sauce. Serves 6 to 8.

Lemon Sauce:

1/4 c. olive oil
2 T. lemon juice
2 T. shallots, chopped
2 T. capers, chopped
1 T. fresh parsley, chopped

1/2 t. dry mustard
1/2 t. garlic, minced
1/4 t. salt
1/8 t. white pepper

Whisk together all ingredients in a small bowl.

A pat of herb butter is heavenly on grilled foods and warm rolls! Blend together softened butter, chopped fresh chives or marjoram and a touch of lemon juice. Roll up in wax paper and chill, then slice to serve.

Butter & Herb Grilled Shrimp

Amy Wrightsel
Louisville, KY

You'll love this buttery shrimp...it's very tasty, quick & easy.

1/2 c. butter
1/4 c. dried parsley
1/4 c. dried chives
2 T. granulated garlic

16 to 20 uncooked jumbo
   shrimp, peeled, cleaned
   and butterflied

Place butter in a disposable 13"x9" aluminum baking pan. Set on a grate over medium heat; allow butter to melt. Add herbs and garlic to pan; mix well. Add shrimp to pan; stir to coat well with butter mixture. Remove pan from grill. Remove shrimp from pan, reserving butter mixture. Oil grate; place shrimp directly on grate. Grill just until shrimp are cooked and pink, about 3 minutes per side. Return shrimp to reserved butter mixture in pan; place pan back on the grill. Cook on grill for an additional 3 to 4 minutes. Serves 4.

Use a grill basket to cook small pieces of meat, fish and veggies...they won't fall through the grate and are much easier to turn for even cooking.

Puddie's Peel & Eat Shrimp

Cris Goode
Mooresville, IN

My husband makes this tasty treat for my extended family over a campfire when we visit Memaw and Papaw at horse camp!

1 T. seasoned salt
1 T. seafood seasoning
1 T. chili powder
1 t. canola oil

12-oz. pkg. frozen uncooked jumbo shrimp, thawed and cleaned

In a large bowl, mix seasonings and oil. Add shrimp and toss to coat; let stand for 20 minutes. Drain, discarding marinade. Place shrimp over medium-high heat. Cook for 5 to 10 minutes, until shrimp are pink. Peel and eat. Serves 4 to 6.

Just for fun, serve an all-finger-food dinner. Serve Puddie's Peel & Eat Shrimp, French fries and fresh carrot and celery dippers with cups of creamy ranch dressing. For dessert, frosty fruit pops or ice cream sandwiches are perfect. Pass the napkins, please!

Grilled Eggplant Parmesan

Amanda Bonagura
Floral Park, NY

A perfect garden recipe...most of the ingredients can go straight from the garden to the grill to the table. This dish pairs well with pasta or polenta and a good red wine.

1 eggplant, peeled and sliced
    into 1/2-inch rounds
1/4 to 1/2 c. extra-virgin
    olive oil
1 to 2 tomatoes, sliced 1/4-inch
    thick, or 15-oz. can crushed
    tomatoes

6 to 7 Kalamata olives, chopped
5 to 10 fresh basil leaves,
    chopped
8-oz. ball fresh mozzarella
    cheese, sliced 1/4-inch thick
salt and pepper to taste
Garnish: additional olive oil

Brush both sides of eggplant slices with olive oil. Place on a vegetable grilling rack over a hot grate. Grill until tender and golden on both sides, about 15 to 20 minutes. Remove eggplant to a large grill-safe baking pan coated with non-stick vegetable spray. Arrange tomatoes over eggplant. Combine olives and basil in a small bowl; spread over tomatoes and top with cheese. Turn off burners on one side of grill; set pan on this side. Cover grill and cook until hot and cheese is bubbly, about 15 minutes. Season with salt and pepper; drizzle with additional olive oil. Serves 4.

For the freshest flavor, store olive oil in the fridge...just pour a little into a small cruet for everyday use. Olive oil thickens when chilled, but will thin quickly at room temperature.

Grilled Vegetable Salad

JoAnn
Gooseberry Patch

I received this terrific recipe from a cooking class.

1 ear corn, husked
16 spears asparagus, trimmed
16 green onions, trimmed
8 roma tomatoes, halved
1 bulb fennel, thinly sliced
2 to 3 T. olive oil

salt and pepper to taste
1 c. couscous, cooked
6-oz. pkg. spring greens
Garnish: chopped fresh basil,
  parsley and/or mint

Place all vegetables in a grill basket. Drizzle with oil; season with salt and pepper. Place basket on a grate over high heat. Cook until tender, about 5 to 10 minutes, turning occasionally. Remove grill basket from grill; cool. Slice corn kernels off cob; cut other vegetables into bite-size pieces. Combine all vegetables in a large salad bowl. Add couscous and greens. Add Vinaigrette to taste; toss to mix. Garnish with herbs. Serves 4 to 6.

Vinaigrette:

1/2 c. olive oil
1/4 c. lemon juice

1 T. Dijon mustard
salt and pepper to taste

Whisk together all ingredients in a bowl, blending well.

A vintage wooden salad bowl is a terrific thrift-shop find. To restore the bowl's glowing finish, sand lightly inside and out with fine sandpaper. Rub a little vegetable oil over the bowl and let stand overnight, then wipe off any excess oil in the morning. It will look like new!

Parsley & Parmesan Potatoes

Melanie Lowe
Dover, DE

My family just loves new potatoes and fresh herbs from the farmers' market when I prepare them this way.

3 lbs. new redskin potatoes
1 c. green onions, sliced thinly
1/4 c. olive oil, divided
3 T. grated Parmesan cheese

3 T. fresh parsley, minced
2 T. fresh oregano, minced
3 cloves garlic, minced
salt and pepper to taste

In a saucepan, cover potatoes with water. Cook over medium-high heat until tender; drain. Let potatoes cool; cut in half and place in a large bowl. Drizzle with 2 tablespoons olive oil and toss well. Place potatoes in a grill basket; season with salt and pepper. Place basket on a grate over medium-high heat. Cook for 5 minutes; stir well and cook another 5 minutes, or until golden. Remove potatoes to a bowl; toss with remaining olive oil and other ingredients. Serve warm.
Serves 6 to 8.

Whip up some fresh stirrers for lemonade, sweet tea or other favorite cookout beverages! Simply thread melon balls onto wooden skewers.

Balsamic Grilled Tomatoes

Amy Hunt
Traphill, NC

These tomatoes are a wonderful side dish for grilled steak. They're tasty and look so pretty on the plate, yet are easy to do.

4 tomatoes, halved
1/4 c. balsamic vinaigrette
    salad dressing

1/4 c. grated Parmesan cheese

Place tomatoes in a disposable 13"x9" aluminum foil baking pan, cut-side up. Drizzle with salad dressing; sprinkle with cheese. Place pan on a grate over medium heat. Cook for 15 minutes, or until tomatoes are soft and cheese is golden. Serves 4.

A vintage-style oilcloth tablecloth with brightly colored fruit and flowers adds cheer to any dinner table. Its wipe-clean ease makes it oh-so practical for cookouts.

Versatile Grilled Veggies

Regina Wickline
Pebble Beach, CA

We love these savory grilled veggies as a hot side dish or as a cool salad topping...they're even yummy in a pita as a light meal!

3/4 lb. mushrooms, trimmed
3/4 lb. cherry tomatoes
1 c. red, yellow or green pepper,
    sliced
1/2 c. red onion, sliced

1/2 c. zucchini, sliced
1/2 c. yellow squash, sliced
1/2 c. olive oil
1/2 c. lemon juice
1/2 c. light soy sauce

Combine vegetables in a large bowl; set aside. In a small bowl, whisk together remaining ingredients; pour over vegetables and toss to mix. Cover and refrigerate for 30 minutes to an hour. Drain, reserving marinade. Place vegetables in a grill basket over medium-high heat. Cook for 12 to 15 minutes, brushing with marinade, until tender. Serve warm or cooled. Makes 6 to 8 servings.

Vintage tin picnic baskets are terrific...so roomy, they easily tote goodies to & from a picnic, wipe clean in a jiffy and can be found in a variety of colors and fun patterns.

Lemony Grilled Broccoli

Erin Brock
Charleston, WV

*Delicious! My picky kid who won't eat steamed broccoli
gobbles it up when it's fixed this way.*

2-1/2 T. lemon juice
2 T. olive oil
1/4 t. salt
1/4 t. pepper

1 bunch broccoli, cut into spears
  and trimmed
3/4 c. grated Parmesan cheese

In a large bowl, whisk together lemon juice, oil, salt and pepper; add broccoli and toss to coat. Let stand for 30 minutes. Toss broccoli again; drain and discard marinade. Place cheese in a large plastic zipping bag. Add broccoli, a few pieces at a time; shake to coat. Grill broccoli, covered, on an oiled grate over medium heat for 8 to 10 minutes on each side, until crisp-tender. Serves 4 to 6.

It's a snap to clean the grate after cooking! A little water and a scouring pad or grill brush will do the trick...a crumpled ball of aluminum foil works well in a pinch too! Rinse the grate well and let dry before storing.

Sizzling Bacon Asparagus

Katie Majeske
Denver, PA

Fresh asparagus in the spring is the best...such a delicacy!

16 spears asparagus, trimmed
2 to 3 t. olive oil

pepper to taste
4 slices bacon

Arrange asparagus on a baking sheet. Lightly drizzle with olive oil; sprinkle with pepper. Make a bundle with 4 spears; wrap in a slice of bacon. Secure with wooden toothpicks, if needed. Repeat with remaining ingredients to make 4 bundles. Place on an oiled grate over medium-high heat. Cook for 10 to 12 minutes, turning occasionally, until asparagus is tender and bacon is crisp. Makes 4 servings.

No more flimsy paper plates...they'll fit nice and snug
inside a plastic flying disc.

Grilled Portabella Blues

Marion Sundberg
Ramona, CA

This is a favorite at all our barbecues. Serve the mushrooms whole alongside grilled meat, or cut them into bite-size pieces and serve as an appetizer.

1/2 c. balsamic vinegar
1/4 c. olive oil
2 cloves garlic, pressed
salt and pepper to taste

4 large portabella mushroom caps
1/2 c. crumbled blue cheese

Mix vinegar, oil, garlic, salt and pepper in a large plastic zipping bag. Add mushrooms; seal bag and refrigerate for at least one hour. Drain, discarding marinade. Grill mushrooms over medium heat until tender and golden. Just before removing mushrooms from grill, spoon blue cheese into the center of each mushroom. Let stand until cheese melts; serve immediately. Makes 4 servings.

Enjoy star-spangled barbecues all summer long! Use red, white & blue tableware along with mini flags tucked into the centerpiece.

Grilled Pepperoni Log

Lori Rosenberg
University Heights, OH

This recipe is a real crowd-pleaser! Pepperoni Logs on the grill have a wonderful smoky taste and are easy to make and clean up.

16-oz. loaf frozen bread dough, thawed
4-oz. pkg. sliced pepperoni
1 c. shredded mozzarella cheese
1/4 c. grated Parmesan cheese
1-1/2 t. Italian seasoning

Preheat grill until hot, about 375 degrees. On a lightly floured surface, roll out thawed bread dough into a 13-inch by 9-inch rectangle. Arrange pepperoni and cheeses evenly over dough. Sprinkle with seasoning. Roll up dough jelly-roll style, starting on one long edge; pinch seam to seal. Place dough seam-side down on grate over indirect heat. Cook for 20 minutes on each side. Slice to serve. Makes 12 to 14 servings.

Make some stepping stones for backyard fun. Stir up ready-mix cement following package instructions and pour it into a plastic-lined pizza box. Let the kids press in their hands or feet and inscribe their names. It'll be such fun at the next family get-together to see how they've grown!

Jalapeño Poppers

Laura Smith
Appleton City, MO

*We tried these yummy peppers on a camping trip
with friends, and everyone loved them. Give it a try...
I guarantee there will be none left!*

20 jalapeño peppers, halved and
    seeds removed
2 8-oz. pkgs. cream cheese,
    softened

1 to 2 16-oz. pkgs. bacon

Fill each jalapeño half with cream cheese; wrap with a bacon slice and fasten with wooden toothpicks. Lay a long piece of aluminum foil on grate over medium heat; arrange peppers cheese-side up on foil. Cook until peppers are tender and bacon is crisp. Allow to cool slightly before serving. Poppers may also be placed on a rimmed baking sheet and baked at 350 degrees for 45 minutes. Serves 8 to 10.

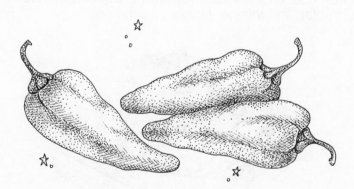

When preparing hot jalapeño peppers, it's always a good idea to wear plastic gloves to avoid irritation while cutting, slicing and chopping. Don't touch your face, lips or eyes while you're working! Just toss away the gloves when you're done.

Stuffed & Grilled Spuds

Wendy Jacobs
Idaho Falls, ID

This is a yummy treat to share with friends! I like to bake the potatoes the day before and mash the scooped-out potato to serve with that night's dinner. Then just pop the skins in the fridge until it's grilling time.

6 russet potatoes
2 to 4 T. butter, melted
salt and pepper to taste
2 c. shredded Cheddar cheese

4 slices bacon, crisply cooked
 and crumbled
Garnish: sour cream, chopped
 green onion and tomato

Pierce potatoes several times with a fork. Brush skins with some of the melted butter, if desired. Bake at 350 degrees for about 60 minutes, until tender. Cut potatoes in half lengthwise. Scoop out pulp to create shells about 1/4-inch thick; reserve pulp for another use. Brush the inside of each shell with butter; season with salt and pepper. Divide cheese and bacon among potato shells. Place on an oiled grate over medium heat for 10 to 12 minutes, until crisp. Cover grill for the last few minutes, until cheese melts. Top with dollops of sour cream and a sprinkle of onion and tomato. Makes 12 servings.

A warm, melting cheese appetizer on the grill is irresistible!
Choose Camembert or another soft cheese. Brush it with olive oil
and place directly on the grill until warmed through, about
two minutes per side. Serve with baguette slices.

Grilled Italiano Spread

Barb Bargdill
Gooseberry Patch

This is such an easy appetizer to prepare at a cookout!

8-oz. pkg. Neufchâtel cheese
1/4 c. basil pesto sauce
1 roma tomato, chopped

1/4 c. finely shredded Italian-
  blend cheese
shredded wheat crackers

Unwrap Neufchâtel cheese and place on a piece of heavy-duty foil. Top with pesto, tomato and shredded cheese. Place foil on grate over medium heat. Cover and grill for 8 to 10 minutes, until shredded cheese is melted and Neufchâtel cheese is softened but still holds its shape. Serve warm with crackers. Serves 10 to 12.

Hot Chili-Sausage Dip

Jill Valentine
Jackson, TN

The whole gang loves this spicy, chunky warm dip...
it's a good thing this recipe makes a lot!

1 lb. Italian ground pork
  sausage
16-oz. can chili
1 clove garlic, minced
1 T. dried oregano

1 c. shredded Cheddar cheese
8-oz. pkg. cream cheese, cubed
  and softened
crusty bread slices or tortilla
  chips

Heat a cast-iron skillet on a grate over medium heat. Add sausage and cook until browned; drain. Stir in chili, garlic and oregano; heat until bubbly. Add cheeses; reduce heat to low or move skillet to indirect heat. Simmer until thickened and cheeses are melted, about 5 minutes. Serve warm with bread or chips. Makes about 4 cups.

Large scallop shells make delightful serving containers for seafood sauces. Use shells you've found on a family beach vacation or check craft supply stores for shells.

Momcy's Grilled Flatbread

Lisa Kastning
Marysville, WA

My mother-in-law's name is Nancy, but I have always called her "Momcy" as she's just like a second mom to me. She has given me many wonderful family-loved recipes. This is one of my favorites!

1/2 c. warm water	3/4 t. salt
1/2 t. active dry yeast	2 T. olive oil, divided
1-1/3 c. all-purpose flour	coarse salt to taste

Heat water until very warm, about 110 to 115 degrees. Combine with yeast in a small bowl; let stand for 5 minutes. In a medium bowl, combine flour and salt. Add yeast mixture and one tablespoon olive oil to flour mixture. Stir to mix; knead until soft dough forms. Cover; let rise for 30 minutes. Divide into 4 balls and roll into rounds, 1/8-inch thick. Lightly coat each side with remaining olive oil. Grill over medium-high heat until crisp and very lightly golden; sprinkle with coarse salt. Makes 4 servings.

Grilled Parmesan Bread

Nancy Molldrem
Eau Claire, WI

Crisp toasted cheesy bread...yum! We make it every time we grill.

1/4 c. butter, softened	6 slices French bread, 1-inch
1/2 c. grated Parmesan cheese	thick, cut on the diagonal

Blend butter and cheese in a small bowl. Spread mixture on both sides of bread slices. Place on a grate over medium heat. Toast until golden, about 3 minutes on each side. Serves 6.

A generous square of red-checked homespun makes a cozy liner for a basket of hot bread.

Mom's Best Burgers

Jacqueline Kurtz
Wernersville, PA

*From my mom's recipe collection...she made these
burgers for special occasions.*

2 lbs. ground beef
1 onion, chopped
1/2 c. Italian-flavored dry
   bread crumbs
1/3 c. teriyaki sauce
1 T. grated Parmesan cheese

1 t. dried basil
1 t. salt
1 t. pepper
6 onion rolls, split
6 slices Cheddar cheese

In a large bowl, combine all ingredients except rolls and cheese. Mix
well and form into 6 patties. Grill over medium-high heat to desired
doneness, about 5 to 7 minutes on each side. Serve burgers on rolls,
topped with cheese. Makes 6 servings.

Spicy Turkey Burgers

Louise Gilbert
British Columbia, Canada

*These delicious turkey burgers always get me great reviews
from my friends! They're a nice change from beef.*

1 lb. ground turkey
1/3 c. quick-cooking oats,
   uncooked
1/2 c. catsup
1 T. vinegar
1 T. Worcestershire sauce

2 cloves garlic, minced
1/4 to 1/2 t. red pepper flakes
1/4 t. hot pepper sauce
1/4 t. pepper
4 hamburger buns, split

Combine turkey and oats in a large bowl; set aside. In a small bowl,
mix together remaining ingredients except buns. Add half of catsup
mixture to turkey mixture; blend thoroughly. Form into 4 patties. Grill
burgers over medium-high heat for 5 to 7 minutes; turn over. Baste
with remaining sauce and grill another 5 to 7 minutes, to desired
doneness. Serve burgers on buns. Makes 4 servings.

Sizzling Herb Burgers

Larraine Trotter
Goldfield, IA

*I have been trying out fun recipes using fresh herbs
from my garden...this one is mmm good!*

3 lbs. ground beef
1 c. Italian-flavored dry
   bread crumbs
3 eggs, beaten
3 cloves garlic, minced
2 T. garlic chives, chopped

2 T. fresh basil, chopped
2 T. fresh flat-leaf parsley,
   chopped
1 t. fresh rosemary, chopped
salt and pepper to taste
8 to 10 hamburger buns, split

In a large bowl, mix together all ingredients except buns. Form into
8 to 10 patties. Grill burgers over medium-high heat to desired
doneness, about 5 to 7 minutes on each side. Serve burgers on buns.
Makes 8 to 10 servings.

Delicious burgers begin with ground beef chuck labeled as 80/20.
A little fat in the beef adds flavor...there's no need to purchase
expensive ground sirloin.

Backyard Cheddar BBQ Burgers

Brandi Bryant
Baton Rouge, LA

My husband and kids love it when Mom grills for a change...these burgers with a tasty secret are a big hit at our house! Everyone goes crazy over them, especially the kids. We make them year 'round.

1 lb. ground beef chuck
1-oz. pkg. ranch salad dressing
   mix
1 t. olive oil
1 c. shredded sharp Cheddar
   cheese

favorite barbecue sauce to taste
10 slices Texas toast
Garnish: favorite condiments

Mix together beef, salad dressing mix and oil in a large bowl. Form into 5 patties. Place a generous pinch of cheese into the center of each patty. Fold in and reshape patties until cheese is hidden inside. Grill burgers over medium heat for 20 minutes; turn. Brush burgers with barbecue sauce and grill for 5 more minutes, until sizzling. Serve burgers on Texas toast, topped with desired condiments. Makes 5 servings.

For the juiciest grilled foods, flip burgers using a spatula, but don't press them down on the grill. Turn steaks, chicken and brats with tongs.

Homemade Burger Buns

Regina Vining
Warwick, RI

Any kind of burger is extra-special served on a fresh-baked bun!
These don't take long to make...why not stir up a batch today?

2 T. active dry yeast
1 c. plus 2 T. warm water
1/3 c. oil
1/4 c. sugar

1 egg, beaten
1 t. salt
3 to 3-1/2 c. all-purpose flour
Optional: melted butter

In a large bowl, dissolve yeast in very warm water, 110 to
115 degrees. Stir in oil and sugar; let stand for 5 minutes. Mix in egg
and salt; stir in enough flour to form a soft dough. Turn onto a floured
surface. Knead for 3 to 5 minutes, until smooth and elastic. Divide
dough into 8 to 12 balls. Place on greased baking sheets, 3 inches
apart. Cover and let stand for 10 minutes. Brush with butter, if desired.
Bake at 425 degrees for 8 to 12 minutes, until golden. Cool buns on
wire racks. Makes 8 to 12 buns.

BBQ Bacon Cheeseburgers

Jenny Bishoff
Mountain Lake Park, MD

My husband came up with this recipe. It's terrific on the grill
and a less messy way to eat bacon cheeseburgers.

6 slices bacon, crisply cooked
    and crumbled
1 lb. ground beef or turkey
1 c. shredded Cheddar cheese

salt and pepper to taste
favorite barbecue sauce to taste
4 hamburger buns, split

In a large bowl, mix together meats, cheese and seasonings. Mix
gently, using your hands. Form into 4 patties. Place on a medium-hot
grill and cook to desired doneness, about 5 to 7 minutes per side. Near
the end of cooking time, baste with barbecue sauce; heat through.
Serve burgers on buns. Makes 4 servings.

Tina's All-Star Sliders on Cornbread Buns

Tina Goodpasture
Meadowview, VA

I was raised on homemade cornbread...it still makes me think of my grandmother's house. The smell makes my mouth water!

3/4 lb. ground beef chuck
1 egg, lightly beaten
1/3 c. onion, chopped
1/3 c. shredded Pepper Jack cheese

1 t. garlic powder
1/4 t. chili powder
1/4 t. salt
hot pepper sauce to taste

In a large bowl, combine all ingredients; mix well. Form into twelve 2-1/2 inch patties. Grill over medium-high heat for 3 to 4 minutes per side. Serve sliders on split Cornbread Buns. Makes 12 servings.

Cornbread Buns:

3/4 c. yellow cornmeal
3/4 c. all-purpose flour
1 T. sugar
2 t. baking powder
3/4 t. salt

1/2 t. pepper
3/4 c. sour cream
2 T. oil
2 eggs, lightly beaten

Combine dry ingredients in a bowl; mix well. Add remaining ingredients; stir just until smooth. Spray a muffin tin with non-stick vegetable spray. Fill muffin cups 3/4 full, spreading batter to edges. Bake at 350 degrees for 8 to 10 minutes, until centers spring back when touched. Cool buns in tin for about 5 minutes; remove to a wire rack. Makes one dozen.

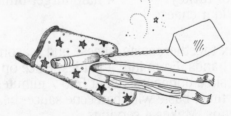

Hickory, mesquite and applewood chips add wonderful smoky flavor to grilled foods. Just soak in water, drain and scatter onto hot coals.

Grilled Portabella Burgers

JoAnn
Gooseberry Patch

So flavorful that you'll never miss the meat!

1/4 c. butter, melted
2 T. fresh basil, chopped
2 T. balsamic vinegar
4 t. garlic, minced
4 large portabella mushroom
  caps

4 slices sweet onion
4 whole-wheat hamburger buns,
  split
4 slices Muenster cheese
Garnish: romaine lettuce, tomato
  slices

Combine butter, basil, vinegar and garlic in a small bowl. Brush butter mixture over mushroom caps and onion slices. Place mushrooms and onion on grill over medium heat. Grill for 4 to 5 minutes on each side, turning once and brushing with remaining butter mixture. Brush remaining butter mixture over cut sides of buns. Grill buns cut-side down for one to 2 minutes, until toasted. Place each mushroom cap on a bun; top with a cheese slice, lettuce and tomato. Makes 4 servings.

Put a new spin on burgers! Swap out the same ol' buns with different types of bread like English muffins, Italian ciabatta or sliced French bread. Pita rounds make sandwiches that are easier for littler hands to hold.

Inside-Out Burgers

Lynda Mayes
Hanscom AFB, MA

My family would all get together every year in Indianapolis over Memorial Day weekend for the big race. One year my godmother made these burgers at our cookout. Her burgers were the best I ever tasted...all the good stuff is hidden inside!

2 to 2-1/2 lbs. ground beef
   sirloin
2 T. Worcestershire sauce
2 T. favorite steak seasoning

1/4 lb. Colby Jack cheese, cubed
6 slices bacon, crisply cooked
   and crumbled
4 hamburger buns, split

Place beef, sauce and seasoning in a large bowl. Mix together, using your hands, just until combined. Divide beef mixture into 2 parts with one part a little larger than the other. Divide larger part into 4 flattened patties; top each with cheese and bacon. Make 4 smaller patties and place on top of larger stuffed patties. Pinch sides to seal well. Grill burgers to desired doneness over medium-high heat, about 6 to 8 minutes per side. Serve burgers on buns. Makes 4 servings.

Serve up cookout meals on thrift-shop enamelware plates, cups and flatware. They're colorful, unbreakable and can go back into the picnic basket, not into the trash.

Eggstravagant Burgers

Sophia Graves
Okeechobee, FL

I first tried this burger at a small diner in central Florida. I would never have thought of putting a fried egg on a burger, but it is oh-so good! So I made my own version with a few added touches.

1 lb. lean ground beef
1 t. garlic, minced
salt and pepper to taste
Optional: 1 c. onion, sliced
Optional: 1 c. green pepper,
    sliced

1 T. butter
4 eggs
4 hamburger buns, split
4 slices Cheddar cheese
Garnish: mayonnaise, mustard,
    catsup

Mix together beef, garlic, salt and pepper in a bowl. Form into 4 patties; grill or pan-fry to desired doneness; keep warm. While burgers are cooking, spray a skillet with non-stick spray. Sauté onion and green pepper, if using, over medium heat until tender. Remove vegetables to a plate. Melt butter in skillet; break eggs into skillet and cook until yolks are set to desired doneness. Place buns on a baking sheet; warm in oven at 350 degrees for 10 minutes. Top each bun with a burger, a cheese slice, a fried egg and a spoonful of vegetable mixture. Garnish with condiments as desired. Serves 4.

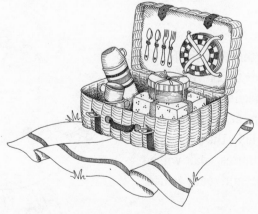

Keep hot foods hot, cold foods cold...don't let picnic food sit out longer than two hours, even if it still looks fine. Wrap and refrigerate any leftovers promptly. Better safe than sorry!

Hawaiian Bar-B-Que Burgers

Cindy McKinnon
El Dorado, AR

These burgers are so good! We love to cook out on our charcoal grill, and this is one of my family's favorites.

2 lbs. ground beef
2 t. Worcestershire sauce
1/2 c. favorite barbecue sauce
1/2 c. pineapple preserves
1 T. brown sugar, packed

20-oz. can sliced pineapple, drained
6 to 8 hamburger buns, split
Optional: lettuce leaves, cheese slices

Combine beef and Worcestershire sauce in a large bowl. Mix thoroughly; form into 6 to 8 patties and set aside. Combine barbecue sauce, preserves and brown sugar in a small saucepan. Bring to a boil over medium heat, stirring frequently. Remove from heat. Brush patties with sauce mixture and place on a grill over medium heat. Cook to desired doneness, 5 to 7 minutes on each side, brushing with sauce mixture after each turn. Meanwhile, brush pineapple slices with sauce mixture and add to grill; cook for 2 minutes on each side. Grill buns. Top each bun with a burger, a pineapple slice, a lettuce leaf, some extra sauce mixture and a cheese slice, if desired. Makes 6 to 8 servings.

A chimney starter is terrific for getting charcoal ready to cook quickly...no lighter fluid needed. Place crumbled newspaper in the bottom, fill with briquets and light the paper. In just 15 to 20 minutes, coals will be glowing hot and ready to use.

Caramelized Onion Burgers

Nancy Girard
Chesapeake, VA

These burgers are the best...everyone loves them! A little tip I learned so you don't get that bump in the center of the burger...make a small indentation in the center, not all the way through. No more bumps!

1 lb. ground beef
1/4 c. fresh parsley, chopped
2 T. tomato paste
2 t. Worcestershire sauce
1/2 t. salt
1/4 t. pepper
4 hamburger buns, split and toasted
Optional: lettuce leaves, tomato slices

Prepare Caramelized Onion Topping; keep warm. Combine beef, parsley, tomato paste, Worcestershire sauce, salt and pepper. Form into 4 patties. Grill over medium heat to desired doneness, 6 to 8 minutes on each side. Serve burgers on buns, topped with spoonfuls of Caramelized Onion Topping and, if desired, lettuce and tomato. Makes 4 servings.

Caramelized Onion Topping:

2 T. olive oil
4 onions, sliced
2 t. sugar
1/4 c. water
1 T. balsamic vinegar
1/4 t. salt

Heat olive oil in a skillet over low heat. Add onions and sprinkle with sugar. Cook over low heat for 20 to 25 minutes, stirring often, until onions are caramelized and golden. Stir in water, vinegar and salt. Serve warm.

Fill empty plastic milk jugs with water, then freeze. Packed in a camp cooler, they'll keep food chilled longer than ice, with no drippy mess.

Spicy Marinated Burgers

Kristin Stone
Little Elm, TX

I created this recipe to give more flavor to burgers made from lean ground meat. Top with a slice of chipotle Cheddar, a few slices of crisp bacon and some BBQ sauce for a real treat!

1/4 c. water
2 T. Worcestershire sauce
1 t. favorite barbecue sauce
1 t. chili powder
1 t. ground cumin
1 t. Cajun seasoning
1/2 t. pepper
1/2 t. red pepper flakes
1/4 t. hot pepper sauce
1/4 t. smoke-flavored cooking
 sauce
1-1/4 lbs. lean ground beef
 or turkey
5 hamburger buns, split

In a large bowl, combine all ingredients except meat and buns. Crumble meat over mixture; mix thoroughly and form into 5 patties. Cover and refrigerate for one hour. Grill to desired doneness over medium-high heat, 5 to 7 minutes per side. Serve on buns. Makes 5 servings.

Tasty Turkey Burgers

Kathleen Sturm
Corona, CA

My family loves these turkey burgers! They are flavorful and never bland, like turkey burgers tend to be.

1 lb. ground turkey
1 T. soy sauce
1 T. catsup
1/4 t. garlic powder
4 to 6 hamburger buns, split
Garnish: favorite condiments

Combine turkey, soy sauce, catsup and garlic powder in a large bowl. Mix together and form into 4 to 6 patties. Grill burgers over medium-high heat for about 5 to 7 minutes on each side. Serve burgers on buns with desired condiments. Serves 4 to 6.

Black Bean Turkey Burgers

Amy Thomason Hunt
Traphill, NC

These burgers are delicious topped with my Avocado & Onion Slaw.
Don't be surprised if you're asked for the recipe!

1-1/4 lbs. ground turkey
3/4 c. canned black beans,
   drained, rinsed and lightly
   mashed
1 c. tortilla chips, crushed

1 T. chili powder
1 T. ground cumin
salt and pepper to taste
6 hamburger buns, split

In a large bowl, combine turkey, beans, tortilla chips and seasonings. Mix well with your hands and form into 6 patties. Grill over medium-high heat for 6 to 8 minutes per side. Serve burgers on buns, topped with a scoop of Avocado & Onion Slaw. Makes 6 servings.

Avocado & Onion Slaw:

3 T. mayonnaise
1 T. vinegar
1/4 t. salt

1 avocado, halved, pitted
   and cubed
1/2 c. onion, thinly sliced

Mix together mayonnaise, vinegar and salt until well combined. Stir in avocado and onion.

Don't overlook the vegetarians at your barbecue! Portabella mushrooms and thick slices of eggplant grill up into bun-filling treats...so much the better if a homemade burger topping like Avocado & Onion Slaw is on the menu. Pita rounds stuffed with grilled veggies are a good choice too.

Chili Pepper Pork Satay

Jenny Nangoy
Austin, TX

Satay is small pieces of meat on skewers roasted on a grill...a dish from Indonesia, where we are used to moderate, hot or very hot food made with chili peppers. It's good with boneless chicken thighs too.

20 shallots or 1 red onion,
   chopped
5 to 10 red chili peppers,
   to taste, or paprika
2-inch slice fresh ginger, peeled
   and chopped
1/2 to 1 T. lime juice
1 t. salt, or to taste

2 to 2-1/2 lbs. pork tenderloin,
   cut into 1-inch by 1/2-inch
   pieces
20 skewers
1 to 2 T. oil
cooked rice
Optional: thinly sliced
   cucumbers

In a blender, process shallots or onion, chili peppers or paprika, ginger, lime juice and salt. Pour mixture over pork in a glass baking dish, stirring to coat well. Cover and refrigerate pork for one to 2 hours. Drain, reserving marinade. Thread pork onto skewers. Grill over a medium-hot charcoal fire until pork is well done. Meanwhile, in a skillet over medium-high heat, stir-fry reserved marinade in oil until vegetables are tender. To serve, remove pork to a serving plate; spread with stir-fried mixture. Serve with cooked rice; garnish with cucumbers, if desired. Makes 10 servings.

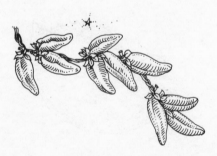

Exotic spices add lots of flavor to grilled foods. Save money by shopping for spices at ethnic groceries, bulk food stores and dollar stores, where they can be quite a bargain.

Pork & Peach Kabobs

Ed Smulski
Lyons, IL

Ripe nectarines and pineapple are luscious with pork too.

2 peaches, halved, pitted and
    cut into 6 wedges
1 sweet onion, cut into 6 wedges
1-1/2 lbs. pork tenderloin, cut
    into 18 to 20 cubes

6 skewers
3/4 c. honey barbecue sauce
Optional: cooked brown rice

Cut peach and onion wedges crosswise in half. Thread peach, onion and pork pieces alternately onto skewers, leaving some space in between for even grilling. Grill skewers over medium-high heat for 15 minutes or until pork juices run clear, turning skewers occasionally. Brush with barbecue sauce during the last 5 minutes. Serve with cooked rice, if desired. Makes 6 servings.

Soak wooden skewers in water for 30 minutes before adding meat and veggies...skewers won't burn on the grill. For even cooking, leave a little space between the pieces on the skewers.

Pineapple Cola Kabobs

Sarah Townsend
Mechanicsville, VA

This is one of the yummiest meals I've ever had! Perfect for get-togethers...it always impresses! Use all beef, or mix it up and use a pound of beef and a pound of chicken.

2 lbs. beef sirloin, cut into
    1-inch cubes
1 fresh pineapple, peeled, cored
    and cut into 1-inch cubes
1-1/4 c. light brown sugar,
    packed
12-oz. can pineapple juice
1/2 c. honey barbecue sauce
1/2 c. steak sauce
1/4 c. soy sauce
1-1/2 t. garlic powder

1 T. onion powder
1 to 2 T. red pepper flakes
1 t. white pepper
10-oz. can cola, chilled
1/2 lb. cherry tomatoes
1 green pepper, cut into squares
1 onion, cut into squares
4 to 6 skewers
Optional: additional barbecue
    sauce, warmed

Combine beef and pineapple in a glass dish; set aside. In a bowl, mix brown sugar, juice, sauces and seasonings. Stir until brown sugar is completely dissolved; slowly pour in cola. Reserve and refrigerate 1/4 cup marinade. Pour remaining marinade over beef mixture; cover and refrigerate for 2 hours to overnight. Drain, discarding marinade. Alternate beef, pineapple and vegetables on skewers. Grill kabobs, uncovered, over medium heat to desired doneness, about 10 minutes, turning occasionally and brushing with reserved marinade. Serve with additional barbecue sauce, if desired. Serves 4 to 6.

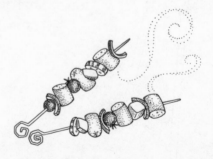

Make kabobs over a tabletop hibachi grill...cozy when it's
just dinner for two.

BURGERS, KABOBS
& MORE

Yummy Meatball Skewers

Sherry Gordon
Arlington Heights, IL

*My kids love these skewers! What's more fun than dinner on a stick?
Sometimes we add cherry tomatoes and zucchini chunks too.*

28-oz. pkg. frozen meatballs,
  thawed
2 green and/or red peppers, cut
  into 1-inch squares
2 c. pineapple cubes

1 red onion, cut into 1-inch
  squares
1-1/2 c. teriyaki sauce
8 to 10 skewers

Place 3 meatballs on each skewer, alternating with pepper, pineapple
and onion pieces. Place skewers on a grill over medium heat. Cook for
10 to 12 minutes, turning skewers occasionally. Brush with sauce
during last 5 minutes of grilling. Serves 8 to 10.

Teriyaki BBQ Beef

Emily Riebold
Milpitas, CA

*This scrumptious recipe has been served at our family picnics,
weddings and other gatherings for 30 years.*

1/2 c. soy sauce
1/2-inch piece fresh ginger,
  peeled and grated
2 T. sugar
1 clove garlic, crushed

3 lbs. beef tri-tip or flank steak,
  thinly sliced into strips
8 skewers
split buns or cooked rice

In a large glass dish, combine sauce, ginger, sugar and garlic. Add
beef; cover and refrigerate at least 30 minutes. Drain, discarding
marinade. Thread beef strips onto skewers. Grill over medium heat to
desired doneness, about 5 to 10 minutes, turning once or twice.
Skewers may also be placed on a rack and broiled for 5 to 10 minutes.
Serve beef on buns or over cooked rice. Serves 8 to 10.

Hawaiian Chicken Kabobs

Emily Hartzell
Portland, IN

Light the tiki torches! This is the perfect recipe for grilling out with family & friends on a balmy summer night.

15-1/4 oz. can pineapple chunks
  in juice, drained and
  1/2 c. juice reserved
1/2 c. soy sauce
1/4 c. canola oil
1 T. brown sugar, packed
2 t. ground ginger
1 t. garlic powder
1 t. dry mustard
1/4 t. pepper

1-1/2 lbs. boneless, skinless
  chicken breasts, cut into
  1-inch cubes
1 lb. bacon, cut into thirds
1 green pepper, cut into
  1-inch squares
12 mushrooms
18 cherry tomatoes
6 skewers
cooked rice

In a small saucepan, stir together reserved pineapple juice, soy sauce, oil, brown sugar and seasonings. Bring to a boil over medium heat; reduce heat and simmer for 5 minutes. Cool slightly. Place chicken in a large shallow glass dish. Pour marinade over chicken; cover and chill for at least one hour. Drain, pouring marinade into a small saucepan; bring to a boil for 3 minutes. Wrap each chicken cube in a piece of bacon. Thread ingredients onto skewers, alternating chicken, pineapple and vegetables. Grill skewers over medium heat for 10 to 15 minutes, brushing often with marinade, until chicken juices run clear. Serve skewers over cooked rice. Makes 6 servings.

Have a kabob party and let your guests make their own. Set out bowls full of sauces, yummy veggies and meats...just watch the skewers fill up!

BURGERS, KABOBS
& MORE

Greek Chicken Kabobs

Lori Rosenberg
University Heights, OH

One of my go-to meals. I like to serve seasoned new potatoes alongside these savory skewers.

1/2 c. Greek vinaigrette salad
   dressing
2 T. mayonnaise
1-1/2 lbs. boneless, skinless
   chicken breasts, cubed

1 red onion, cut into thin
   wedges
4 skewers

Combine dressing and mayonnaise in a bowl; spoon into a large plastic zipping bag. Add chicken; seal bag and turn to coat. Refrigerate for 20 minutes to 2 hours. Remove chicken from bag, discarding marinade. Thread chicken and onion alternately onto skewers. Grill over medium-high heat, turning occasionally, for 8 to 10 minutes, until chicken is cooked through. Serves 4.

Brandie's Chicken Skewers

Brandie Skibinski
Salem, VA

I started making this many years ago for get-togethers with friends. It has been a requested favorite ever since!

1 c. olive oil
3/4 c. soy sauce
1/2 c. lemon juice
1/4 c. mustard
1/4 c. Worcestershire sauce
2 t. garlic, minced

1-1/2 t. pepper
6 boneless, skinless chicken
   breasts, cut into 1-inch strips
   or cubes
4 skewers

In a bowl, mix all ingredients except chicken. If desired, process mixture in a blender until smooth. Place chicken in a shallow glass dish; add marinade and turn to coat well. Cover and refrigerate for 4 hours to overnight. Drain, discarding marinade. Thread chicken onto skewers. Grill over medium-high heat for 5 minutes per side, or until chicken juices run clear. Serves 4.

Firecracker Shrimp

Gail Blain Prather
Stockton, KS

This recipe can be prepared from start to finish in less than 30 minutes! I especially like to make it for company...it turns out wonderful, and I get to spend time with my guests. Serve with a crisp green salad and a loaf of crusty bread.

1/2 c. apricot preserves
1 t. oil
1 t. soy sauce
1/2 t. red pepper flakes

24 large shrimp, peeled
   and cleaned
6 8-inch skewers

In a bowl, combine preserves, oil, soy sauce and red pepper flakes; mix well. Thread 4 shrimp onto each skewer. Brush shrimp with apricot mixture. Grill over medium heat for 2 to 3 minutes per side, or until shrimp are pink and cooked through. Serves 4 to 6.

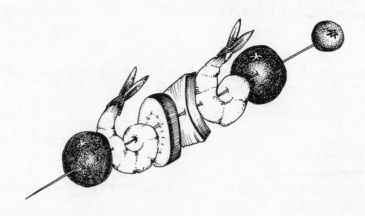

Shrimp kabobs won't slip and twirl if the skewer is inserted through both sides of each shrimp.

Fish-Ka-Bobs

Emily Martin
Ontario, Canada

*Lately my husband and I have been trying to eat more fish.
These skewers are easy and delicious!*

1-1/2 lbs. salmon or halibut
    fillets, sliced into 1-1/2 inch
    thick strips
4 to 6 skewers
1 c. olive oil & vinegar salad
    dressing

2 T. lemon juice
1/4 c. fresh Italian parsley,
    chopped
1 T. fresh rosemary, chopped

If using salmon, remove and discard skin. Thread fish strips onto skewers. Place skewers in a shallow glass dish. Whisk together remaining ingredients in a bowl; drizzle over fish. Cover and refrigerate 30 minutes, turning skewers occasionally. Drain, discarding marinade. Place skewers on a lightly oiled grill over high heat. Cover and cook for 4 minutes per side, or until fish flakes easily with a fork. Makes 4 to 6 servings.

Garlic fans will love the smoky, mellow flavor of garlic roasted on the grill. Trim the top off a head of garlic and set it on a piece of aluminum foil. Add olive oil and salt to taste. Wrap up in the foil and grill over high heat for about 30 minutes, until very soft. To serve, squeeze out the softened cloves onto crusty bread...yum!

BBQ Chicken & Pepper Pizza

Jo-Anne Bougie
Ontario, Canada

A dollop of barbecue sauce adds extra zip to this flavorful pizza.

12-inch pre-baked Italian pizza
   crust
15-oz. can pizza sauce
2 T. favorite barbecue sauce
1 c. cooked chicken, shredded

1 c. shredded mozzarella cheese
1/3 c. green pepper, diced
1/3 c. red pepper, diced
1/3 c. yellow pepper, diced

Preheat grill to medium heat. Place pizza crust on grill; cook for
5 minutes, or until bottom of crust is lightly golden. Combine sauces
in a bowl; spread over crust. Top with chicken, cheese and peppers.
Return to grill for another 5 minutes, or until warmed through and
cheese is melted. Cut into wedges. Makes 6 servings.

Grill up a salad! Choose small heads of romaine or slice larger ones
in half lengthwise; don't separate the leaves. Rinse, pat dry and spritz
with olive oil. Grill over high heat for 2 to 3 minutes per side, until lightly
wilted and golden. Serve lettuce drizzled with balsamic vinaigrette,
or chop and use in a Caesar salad.

Grilled Fresh Summer Pizza

Sonia Daily
Rochester, MI

Fresh basil and ripe tomatoes from my local farmers' market make this recipe a standout! Best of all, it makes two pizzas, so there is plenty to share.

2 12-inch pre-baked Italian
    pizza crusts
6-1/2 oz. container garlic & herb
    spreadable cream cheese
2 roma tomatoes, thinly sliced
1/2 red onion, chopped

8 slices bacon, crisply cooked
    and crumbled
olive oil to taste
8-oz. pkg. shredded mozzarella
    cheese
1/2 c. fresh basil, chopped

Preheat grill to medium heat. Spread cream cheese over pizza crusts. Top with tomatoes, onion and bacon. Drizzle with oil and sprinkle with mozzarella cheese. Place pizzas on grill and reduce to low heat. Cover and cook for 5 to 8 minutes, until crusts are golden and cheese is melted. Remove from grill; top with basil and cut into wedges. Makes 12 servings.

Napkins are a must at cookouts. Cloth napkins are so much nicer than paper ones...why not whip up some fun napkin rings for them? Stitch a pretty silk flower onto colorful new hair elastics...done in a snap!

Charcoal Grilled Pizza

Laura Bice
Columbus, OH

*My husband James is the master griller at our house. He says
it takes trial & error to determine the grilling time and varies
greatly depending on the grill. But it's so worth the effort!*

2 links Italian pork sausage
1 green pepper, halved
1 white onion, halved
1 portabella mushroom cap
2 12-inch pre-baked Italian
   pizza crusts

15-oz. can pizza sauce
2 c. shredded mozzarella cheese
1/4 c. fresh basil, chopped
1/4 lb. pepperoni slices

Build a small charcoal fire in a grill with 12 to 15 charcoal briquets.
Once coals are red-hot, place sausage links on grate over direct heat.
Place green pepper, onion and mushroom cap over indirect heat. Grill,
turning occasionally, until sausages are no longer pink in the center
and vegetables are very tender. Remove sausages and vegetables to a
plate. Cool; cut into bite-size pieces. Meanwhile, place crusts on baking
sheets. Bake at 450 degrees for 5 to 7 minutes, until lightly golden.
Spread crusts with sauce; add sausage-vegetable mixture, cheese, basil
and pepperoni. With a fire tool or a stick, spread coals evenly into a
circle the same diameter as the pizzas. Remove one pizza from baking
sheet to grate. Cover grill, with vents open. Cook until cheese is melted
and bottom of crust is dark golden, about 2 to 10 minutes. Repeat with
second pizza. Makes 2 pizzas, 6 servings each.

White-washed clay pots planted
with fragrant herbs make classic
cookout table centerpieces.

Grilled Grecian Salad Pizza

Lisa Kastning
Marysville, WA

Such a fun pizza! I make it for my sister-in-law who's a vegetarian, but no one misses the meat anyway. Serve it as a main dish or cut into smaller portions to serve as an appetizer.

3 T. olive oil, divided
4 cloves garlic, minced
3 c. romaine lettuce, shredded
1 T. lemon juice
2 12-inch pre-baked Italian
   pizza crusts

2 to 3 tomatoes, thinly sliced
1-1/2 c. crumbled feta cheese
6 to 8 pepperoncini, chopped
1 c. chopped black olives
2 T. fresh oregano, minced
cracked pepper to taste

Heat 1-1/2 tablespoons olive oil in a large skillet over medium heat. Add garlic; sauté until lightly golden. Add lettuce and lemon juice to skillet; stir quickly, just until lettuce is wilted. Brush remaining olive oil over pizza crusts. Top with tomatoes, lettuce mixture and remaining ingredients. Place pizzas on grill over medium-high heat; close cover. Cook until crusts are golden, vegetables are heated through and cheese is beginning to melt. Cut into wedges. Makes 12 to 16 servings.

Invite your friends and neighbors to a good old-fashioned block party. Set up picnic tables, arrange lots of chairs in the shade and invite everyone to bring a favorite dish. Whether it's a summer cookout or a fall harvest party, you'll make some wonderful memories together!

Michelle's BBQ Grilled Meatloaf

Michelle Vandergrift
Drayden, MD

*Flavorful and packed with veggies...this recipe has evolved
as I try to make healthier food choices that are still tasty!*

2 T. olive oil
1 onion, finely chopped
1 t. garlic, minced
8-oz. pkg. mushrooms, finely
   chopped
1 to 2 carrots, peeled and finely
   chopped
3 slices whole-wheat bread,
   torn into small pieces

2 lbs. ground beef
1 egg, beaten
1-1/2 t. salt
1/2 t. pepper
1 c. favorite sweet barbecue
   sauce, divided
1 T. brown sugar, packed
1 T. cider vinegar
1 T. mustard

In a large skillet, heat olive oil over medium heat. Add onion, garlic,
mushrooms and carrots. Cook until softened, about 10 minutes. In a
large bowl, combine vegetable mixture with bread; add beef, egg, salt,
pepper and 1/2 cup barbecue sauce. Mix thoroughly. Form into an
8"x4" meatloaf and place in a mesh grill pan. In a small bowl, combine
remaining barbecue sauce, brown sugar, cider and mustard. Mix well
and spoon over meatloaf. Place grill pan on grill over medium heat.
Cook over indirect heat for about one hour, until internal temperature
reaches 160 degrees on a meat thermometer. Meatloaf may also be
placed in an ungreased 8"x4" loaf pan; bake at 350 degrees for
1-1/2 hours. Makes 8 servings.

Hosting a backyard gathering? Fill
a child's little red wagon with ice
and tuck in bottles of soda and
lemonade. Use colorful ribbon
to tie a bottle opener to
the handle so it stays
near the drinks.

E-Z Home Fries & Eggs

Denise Evans
Moosic, PA

Breakfast cooked in a skillet over a campfire...what a wonderful way to start the day! Speed things up by cooking the potatoes at home to pack in your cooler. Delicious served on toasted English muffins.

2 onions, chopped
1 to 2 t. oil
4 slices bacon, cut into 1-inch
    pieces

8 potatoes, cooked and diced
4 eggs
pepper, paprika and/or dried
    parsley to taste

In a cast-iron skillet over medium heat, cook onions in oil until tender and golden. Remove onions to a plate and set aside. Add bacon to skillet; cook until crisp. Remove bacon to same plate, reserving drippings in skillet. Add potatoes; cook just until golden. Return onions and bacon to skillet; heat through. Crack eggs over potato mixture. Gently toss mixture until eggs are cooked to desired doneness. Add desired seasonings. Serves 4.

Get your campfire started and ready for cooking quickly! Crumple newspaper for the first layer, then add dry twigs. Light the paper, add wood and let it burn until you get red glowing coals. Let it burn down a bit more, then place the cooking grate over the coals.

Blackberry Skillet Pancake

Tina George
El Dorado, AR

When I was a little girl, my brothers and I picked blackberries whenever we visited our great-aunt. She had lots of recipes to use up the berries...this is one of them! I have served this for breakfast alongside scrambled eggs & bacon and even as a dessert.

2/3 c. all-purpose flour	1/2 t. vanilla extract
1/3 c. sugar	1 t. shortening
1/4 t. salt	2 c. blackberries
1 c. milk	3 T. powdered sugar
2 eggs	

Combine flour, sugar and salt in a bowl; stir well. Add milk, eggs and vanilla; whisk until smooth. Heat a cast-iron skillet over medium heat until hot and a drop of water sizzles. Brush skillet with shortening. Reduce heat to low; pour batter into skillet. Cover and cook for 10 minutes, until top is firm and puffy and bottom is golden. With a thin spatula, loosen pancake around sides and carefully slide onto a serving dish. Top with blackberries and sprinkle with powdered sugar. Cut into wedges. Serves 6.

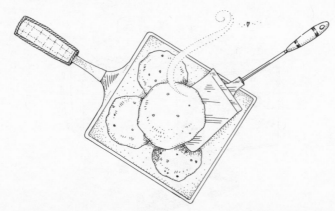

Campers will wake right up for a breakfast pizza! Brush a prebaked pizza crust with olive oil and grill on one side until toasty. Turn over and top with lightly scrambled eggs, crumbled bacon and a handful of cheese. Cover and cook for a few more minutes, until cheese is melted. Yummy!

Dutch Oven Breakfast

Ellie Brandel
Milwaukie, OR

With this hearty breakfast over the campfire, the family is sure to roll right out of the tent as soon as they smell the bacon cooking!

1 lb. bacon, cut into 1-inch
   pieces
32-oz. pkg. frozen diced
   potatoes, plain or with
   onions and peppers, thawed

10 to 16 eggs, beaten
8-oz. pkg. shredded Cheddar
   cheese

Cook bacon in a Dutch oven over a medium-hot campfire. With a slotted spoon, remove bacon to a plate and set aside, reserving one to 2 tablespoons drippings in Dutch oven. Add potatoes and cook until golden. Sprinkle bacon over potatoes. Pour eggs over potato mixture. Place lid on Dutch oven and add several hot coals on top of lid, keeping heat on bottom fairly low. Cook eggs to desired doneness; sprinkle with cheese. Remove oven from campfire; replace lid and let stand until cheese melts. Serves 8.

Nothing is quite as intoxicating as the smell of bacon frying
in the morning, save perhaps the smell of coffee brewing.

– James Beard

Omelet in a Bag

Carol Stepp
Dennison, IL

My son brought home this fun recipe when he was in grade school. We've enjoyed it often while camping in the Smoky Mountains. Fixing eggs for a crowd is a snap! Just set out the ingredients and guests can assemble their own. The omelets can even be wrapped in tortillas for breakfast burritos.

2 eggs
mushrooms, green pepper and/
 or onion, diced and sautéed
green chiles and/or black olives,
 diced

bacon, sausage or ham, chopped
 and browned
shredded cheese

Fill a Dutch oven with water; bring to a boil. Meanwhile, have each person write his or her name with permanent pen on a quart-size plastic zipping freezer bag. Break 2 eggs into bag and squeeze bag to scramble. Add about 1/2 cup of desired ingredients. Press the air out of bag; seal well. Carefully add bag to boiling water; several bags may be cooked at once. Boil for 13 to 15 minutes. Use tongs to remove bag from water. Open carefully and slide omelet out onto a plate. Makes one serving.

The kids will love making cinnamon twists on a stick! Separate refrigerated biscuits and roll them between the hands into long ropes. Wind around a long green stick. Hold over hot coals until golden. Butter well and sprinkle generously with cinnamon-sugar...yum!

Campers' Breakfast

Tammy Burnett
Springfield, MO

When we go camping, we often have a big group of 20 to 25 family members. This breakfast feeds lots of us! Add whatever veggies you like...these are ones we always seem to have on hand. Yum!

1 lb. bacon, chopped
2 green and/or red peppers,
   diced
2 c. onion, diced
12 potatoes, sliced or diced

salt and pepper to taste
1 doz. eggs
1/4 c. water
2 c. shredded Cheddar cheese

In a campfire ring, set a Dutch oven over 15 to 18 hot briquets until heated. Add bacon; cook until crisp and golden. Add peppers and onion; cook until onion is translucent. Push half of the briquets to one side; set Dutch oven on remaining briquets. Add potatoes; season with salt and pepper. Cover Dutch oven with lid; place about 14 briquets on top of lid. Cook for 30 minutes, or until potatoes are tender. Whisk together eggs and water; pour over potatoes. Cover, adding more hot briquets to lid as needed. Cook another 15 to 20 minutes, stirring every 5 minutes, until eggs are set. Top with cheese; cover and let stand until cheese is melted. Serves 12 to 15.

Cowboy coffee...perfect for a chilly morning! Combine ground coffee and cold water in a pot, using one teaspoon of coffee for each cup of water. Bring to a rolling boil; remove from heat; let stand for 3 minutes. Add a tablespoon or two of cold water and the coffee grounds will settle right to the bottom.

Over-the-Fire Breakfast Bake

Peggy Quinton
Louisville, KY

Nothing tastes as good as cooking over an open fire early in the morning with a strong cup of coffee! This is a favorite my husband makes when we're camping. We love it so much we make it at home too. Enjoy...and help yourself to seconds!

6 potatoes, peeled and diced
1/2 c. butter
1 onion, diced
12-oz. can spiced luncheon
    meat, diced

4 eggs
salt and pepper to taste
toast or sourdough bread

Set aside potatoes, covered in water to prevent darkening. In a large cast-iron skillet, melt butter over medium heat. Drain potatoes very well; add to skillet along with onion and meat. Cook until potatoes are golden and tender, stirring often. Use a spoon to make 4 wells in potato mixture. Crack eggs evenly into wells; add salt and pepper to taste. Cover and cook eggs to desired doneness. Serve with toast or bread. Makes 8 to 10 servings.

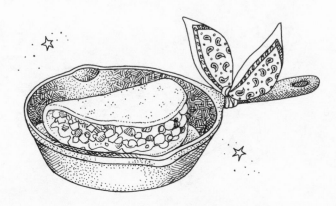

Surprise sleepyheads at breakfast...serve each person a made-to-order omelet in a mini cast-iron skillet. A cheery red bandanna tied around the handle makes a nice big napkin.

Ramsey's Mexican Casserole

*Alice Hardin
Antioch, CA*

This is a great simple one-dish meal! The recipe was given to us by a good friend, a co-worker with whom we used to go camping.

1-1/2 lbs. lean ground beef
1 onion, chopped
1 t. garlic, minced
pepper, garlic powder, chili
   powder and/or ground
   cumin to taste

8-oz. can green chile salsa
16-oz. can stewed tomatoes
7-oz. can diced green chiles
12-oz. pkg. corn chips
16-oz. pkg. shredded Monterey
   Jack cheese

In a large skillet or Dutch oven over medium-high heat, brown beef, onion and garlic. Drain; add desired seasonings. Stir in salsa and tomatoes and chiles with juice. Cover and simmer over medium-low heat for 30 minutes. Top with corn chips and cheese. Cover and let stand to allow cheese to melt. Serves 4 to 6.

One-dish dinners are perfect for campfire cookouts. Save time by chopping veggies at home and placing them in small bags for the cooler. Or choose a recipe using mostly canned ingredients...don't forget the can-opener!

Kicked-Up Campfire Beans

*Amanda Johnson
Marysville, OH*

A fantastic spicy meatless recipe to enjoy around the campfire or backyard fire pit. Adjust the spice to suit your taste.

32-oz. pkg. dried pinto beans
2 red peppers, finely diced
1 onion, finely diced
5 cloves garlic, minced
2 t. chili powder
2 t. salt

2 t. coarse pepper
1 t. cayenne pepper
1 t. ground cumin
1 T. Worcestershire sauce
Optional: 2 t. hot pepper sauce

Cover beans with water in a Dutch oven. Bring to a boil over high heat; reduce to low. Cover and simmer for 2 hours, adding more water as needed. Add peppers, onion and garlic. Cover; cook for another one to 2 hours, adding water as needed. Stir in seasonings and sauces. Simmer an additional 30 to 40 minutes, until thickened and beans are tender. Serves 6.

Stuffed Beer Brats

*Staci Prickett
Montezuma, GA*

I got this recipe from my dad. He didn't often cook for us, but when he did, dinner always seemed extra delicious.

1/4 c. butter, sliced
1 onion, sliced
6 bratwurst sausages
12-oz. can regular or
   non-alcoholic beer

15-oz. can sauerkraut, drained
6 slices bacon
6 hot dog buns, split
Garnish: Swiss cheese slices,
   horseradish mustard

Melt butter in a Dutch oven over medium heat. Add onion; cook for 3 minutes. Add brats and beer; bring to a boil. Reduce heat; simmer for 5 to 10 minutes. Remove brats to a plate, reserving beer mixture. Cut a V-shaped notch lengthwise in brats. Stuff with sauerkraut; wrap with bacon and fasten with a wooden toothpick. Grill over medium heat until golden and bacon is crisp. Return brats to beer mixture until served. Serve on buns, garnished as desired. Serves 6.

Girl Scout Goulash

Elizabeth Ellis
Bangs, TX

This is adapted from one of my Girl Scout troop's favorite camping recipes. So easy to fix...so good to eat on cold evenings!

1 lb. ground beef
1 onion, chopped
salt and pepper to taste
8-oz. can tomato sauce

15-oz. can spaghetti in tomato sauce
15-oz. can ranch-style beans
15-oz. can corn

Brown beef and onion in a skillet over medium heat. Drain; season with salt and pepper. Add all cans, undrained, to skillet; stir. Cook over low heat for 25 to 30 minutes; stir occasionally. Serves 6.

Pan-Fried Corn Fritters

Kelly Alderson
Erie, PA

Delicious with campfire chili!

1 c. biscuit baking mix
8-3/4 oz. can corn, drained
1 egg, beaten

1/4 c. water
1 to 2 T. oil or bacon drippings
Garnish: butter, maple syrup

Combine biscuit mix, corn, egg and water in a bowl; stir well. Grease a cast-iron skillet with oil or drippings. Drop batter into skillet by 1/4 cupfuls. Cook over medium-low heat for about 5 minutes on each side, until golden. Serve warm with butter or syrup. Makes 6 to 8 fritters.

An old oven rack makes a handy grate for cooking over a campfire. Prop it on several logs or large stones.

Brunswick Stew

Patricia Pitcairn
Newtown Square, PA

My mother-in-law made this for my husband and me when I first met her. Everyone who has tasted it asks for the recipe! Served with crusty bread and a tossed salad, it's very satisfying.

2 to 3 T. oil
3 lbs. boneless, skinless chicken
    breasts, cubed
3 10-3/4 oz. cans chicken
    gumbo soup

16-oz. pkg. frozen shoepeg corn
1/3 c. Worcestershire sauce
1 clove garlic, minced

Heat oil in a large deep skillet over medium heat; add chicken. Cook until golden and nearly cooked through; drain. Combine remaining ingredients in a large bowl. Stir; add to chicken. Bring to a boil; reduce heat to low. Continue to cook for 20 minutes, stirring occasionally. Serves 8.

Bake cornbread in a Dutch oven. Grease the inside of an 8" Dutch oven; cover and set on a bed of hot coals to warm. Mix an 8-1/2 ounce box of cornbread mix, one egg and 1/3 cup milk. Pour batter into Dutch oven; cover and return it to the coals. Place 12 to 14 hot coals on lid. Bake for 20 to 30 minutes, until golden, turning occasionally to ensure even baking. Double recipe for a 10" Dutch oven. Pass the butter!

Mom's German Potato Soup

Sandy Coffey
Cincinnati, OH

*We love to try different soups in fall and winter. This one is
a big favorite. Grab a cup and sit by the fire with us!*

2 T. butter
2 onions, chopped
2 cloves garlic, minced
3 stalks celery, thinly sliced
3 potatoes, diced

2 14-oz. cans chicken broth
1-1/2 c. milk
salt and pepper to taste
1 c. shredded Longhorn cheese

Melt butter in a Dutch oven over medium-high heat. Sauté onions,
garlic and celery for 3 to 5 minutes. Add potatoes and chicken broth.
Simmer, uncovered, for about 30 minutes, stirring often, until
vegetables are very tender. Remove soup from heat. Add soup to a
blender, 1/3 at a time, and process until smooth. (Or mash with a
potato masher.) Return soup to Dutch oven. Stir in milk; season with
salt and pepper. Reheat but do not boil. Serve individual bowls
sprinkled with cheese. Makes 6 servings.

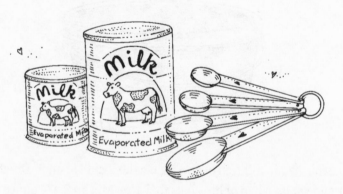

If you enjoy creamy soups, try substituting canned evaporated milk
for half-and-half or whole milk. It doesn't need refrigeration
and is lower in fat too.

Chilly Day Chili

Karen Turner
Ellington, MO

This is a recipe I have changed up over the years...it has become a favorite in our household. It's always a big hit at deer camp!

1 lb. ground beef
15-oz. can Mexican chili beans
15-oz. can pinto beans
15-oz. can red beans
2 8-oz. cans tomato sauce
14-1/2 oz. can diced tomatoes
    with green chiles, puréed
1/4 c. dried, chopped onion

2 T. chili seasoning mix
2 T. chunky salsa
4 to 5 dashes Worcestershire
    sauce
3 dashes hot pepper sauce
1/8 t. garlic powder
garlic salt and pepper to taste

In a large Dutch oven over medium heat, brown beef. Drain; add remaining ingredients. Simmer for 10 to 20 minutes, stirring occasionally. Makes 6 servings.

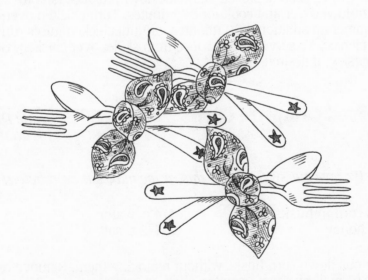

Serve up Chilly Day Chili chuck wagon style. Spoon chili into enamelware bowls, add a side of cornbread and keep bandannas on hand for terrific lap-size napkins.

Skillet BBQ Chicken

Gail Blain Prather
Hastings, NE

A family favorite that uses pantry staples and my beloved cast-iron skillet. I love that it all goes into one skillet and doesn't require a lot of prep. Perfect for busy-night suppers!

2 to 3 T. olive oil
4 chicken breasts, boneless
    or bone-in
1 onion, sliced
2/3 c. catsup
2/3 c. water
3 T. red wine vinegar

3 T. brown sugar, packed
1 T. Worcestershire sauce
1 t. chili powder
1/2 t. dry mustard
1/2 t. celery seed
Optional: chopped fresh parsley

In a large cast-iron skillet, heat oil over medium-high heat. Brown chicken on both sides; remove to a plate. Add onion to skillet; sauté until tender. Stir in remaining ingredients except garnish; bring to a boil. Return chicken to skillet, skin-side down. Reduce heat to medium-low; cover and cook for 30 minutes. Turn chicken over; cover and simmer an additional 20 minutes, or until chicken juices run clear when pierced. To serve, spoon sauce from skillet over chicken. Garnish with parsley, if desired. Serves 4.

Honeyed Campfire Corn

Dale Duncan
Waterloo, IA

We love our sweet corn...this recipe makes it even better!

8 ears corn in husks
1/2 c. honey

1/4 c. water
2-1/2 t. salt

Gently pull down corn husks without removing them. Remove corn silk. In a small saucepan, combine honey, water and salt. Bring to a boil; boil gently for 3 minutes. Brush honey mixture over corn; pat husks back into place. Wrap each ear in aluminum foil. Place wrapped corn in campfire coals. Cook, turning often, until corn is tender, about 20 minutes. Unwrap carefully. Makes 8 servings.

GATHER 'ROUND THE CAMPFIRE

Hungarian Barbecued Wieners

Marcia Shaffer
Conneaut Lake, PA

This recipe was handed down to me by my 82-year-old neighbor who is Hungarian. Every time I serve these wieners, I celebrate our friendship of over 40 years. They're a favorite on the 4th of July... so easy for kids to serve themselves when they come back from swimming in the lake. Happy eating!

2 T. butter
1 lb. hot dogs
1/3 c. green pepper, finely
    chopped
1/3 c. onion, finely chopped
10-3/4 oz. can tomato soup

2 T. brown sugar, packed
1 T. Worcestershire sauce
1 T. vinegar
1 T. mustard
8 hot dog buns, split

Melt butter in a skillet over medium heat. Add hot dogs, green pepper and onion; cook until hot dogs are browned. Stir in remaining ingredients. Cover; simmer for 30 minutes, stirring occasionally. Serve hot dogs on buns, topped with some of the sauce from skillet. Makes 8 servings.

A salt scrub is the best way to clean cast iron...it cleans thoroughly while leaving the pan's seasoning intact. Simply scrub the skillet or Dutch oven with coarse salt and wipe with a soft sponge, then rinse well and pat dry.

Basque Vegetable Soup

Mary Hall
Peoria, IL

A very hearty, satisfying soup that's chock-full of veggies...
this recipe makes enough for a crowd!

2 to 3-lb. chicken
8 c. water
2 carrots, peeled and sliced
1 onion, chopped
1 clove garlic, minced
2 leeks, trimmed and sliced
1 turnip, peeled and cubed
1 potato, peeled and cubed

1 T. fresh parsley, chopped
1 t. dried thyme
salt and pepper to taste
3/4 lb. smoked Polish pork or
   turkey sausage, sliced
1 c. cabbage, shredded
2 c. canned Great Northern
   beans, drained and rinsed

Place chicken in a large Dutch oven; add water. Bring to a boil over medium-high heat. Reduce heat to low and simmer until tender, about 45 minutes. Remove chicken to a plate to cool, reserving broth. Strain broth to skim off fat. Add remaining ingredients except chicken, sausage, cabbage and beans to broth in Dutch oven. Bring to a boil; reduce heat to low and simmer for 30 minutes. Meanwhile, brown sausage in a skillet over medium heat; drain and add to Dutch oven. Remove chicken from bones; cut chicken into bite-size pieces. Add chicken to Dutch oven along with cabbage and beans. Simmer, uncovered, for another 30 minutes, or until vegetables are tender. Serves 10 to 12.

Add some dumplings to your kettle of soup.
To serve six, combine 1-2/3 cups biscuit
baking mix and 2/3 cup milk in a plastic
zipping bag. Squeeze to mix well. Drop
large spoonfuls of batter into simmering
soup. Cover and cook for about 15 minutes,
until dumplings are set.

GATHER 'ROUND THE CAMPFIRE

Kielbasa Camp Stew

Vici Randolph
Gaffney, SC

I love this recipe! It is so simple, but filling and delicious. This stew is terrific with some crusty bread or cornbread!

1 lb. Kielbasa sausage, cut into 1-inch slices
3 14-1/2 oz. cans diced tomatoes
2 12-oz. pkgs. frozen shoepeg corn

4 potatoes, peeled and diced
1/2 head cabbage, coarsely chopped
1 t. Cajun seasoning or other spicy seasoning
salt to taste

Combine Kielbasa, undrained tomatoes and remaining ingredients in a Dutch oven; cover with water. Simmer over medium-high heat until potatoes are tender, stirring occasionally, about 30 minutes. Makes 6 to 8 servings.

They caught fish, cooked supper and ate it...when the shadows of the night closed them in, they gradually ceased to talk and sat gazing into the fire, with their minds evidently wandering elsewhere.

– Mark Twain

Ham & Bean Soup

Kris Thompson
Ripley, NY

This soup is especially good simmered over a campfire in a cast-iron kettle. We enjoy it ladled over slices of cornbread or white bread.

2 c. dried navy beans
6 c. water
1 meaty ham bone
1 onion, chopped
1 carrot, peeled and shredded

1/4 t. garlic powder
1/4 t. dry mustard
1 t. salt
1/2 t. pepper

In a large Dutch oven, cover beans with water. Soak for 8 hours to overnight. Drain well; add 6 cups fresh water and remaining ingredients except salt. Bring to a boil over medium heat. Reduce heat to low. Cover and simmer for 3 to 3-1/2 hours, until beans are tender. Remove ham bone; cool and cut ham from bone. Add ham to soup, discarding bone. Stir in salt. If a smoother soup is desired, mash beans with a potato masher. Makes 6 to 8 servings.

Going camping or hosting a bonfire? Make it easy by preparing soup, stew or chili ahead of time. Just freeze in plastic zipping bags and keep in a cooler, then thaw and reheat over the fire for a quick meal. Soup always tastes even better the next day anyway!

Grandma's Green Bean Dinner

Cathy Loghry
Gun Barrel City, TX

Every summer in Ohio, my Grandpa Ogden grew a garden. Grandma made the most delicious meals with all the fresh produce he grew. This recipe was one of my favorites...she always served it with sliced tomatoes, coleslaw and cornbread. Whenever I make this meal for my family, I think fondly of times spent at their home.

2 lbs. green beans, trimmed
salt and pepper to taste
Optional: 1 T. bacon drippings

3 c. redskin potatoes, cubed
2 c. cooked ham, cubed

Place beans in a Dutch oven. Cover with water and bring to a boil over medium-high heat. Add salt pepper and bacon drippings, if using. Reduce heat to low and simmer for 30 minutes. Add potatoes and ham. Simmer an additional 30 to 45 minutes, until vegetables are tender. Drain before serving. Makes 6 to 8 servings.

Make some quick & easy fire starters to take along to camp. Fold sheets of newspaper into 6-inch squares and secure with natural twine. To use, tuck one under firewood and light with a match...so simple.

Boiled Shrimp in Beer

Vickie
Gooseberry Patch

Treat yourself to these super-easy peel & eat shrimp...even clean-up is a snap! Dump shrimp onto a picnic table covered with newspaper, then after dinner, just toss the paper, shells & all.

1 qt. water
12-oz. can regular or
   non-alcoholic beer
1 lemon, sliced
1 onion, chopped
1 stalk celery, diced

1 T. seafood seasoning
2 bay leaves
hot pepper sauce to taste
1 lb. uncooked large shrimp,
   cleaned
Garnish: cocktail sauce

Combine all ingredients except shrimp and garnish in a Dutch oven. Bring to a boil over medium-high heat. Add shrimp; cover and return to a full boil for 3 to 4 minutes. Stir; remove from heat. Let stand 3 to 4 additional minutes, until shrimp turn pink. Drain well; discard bay leaves. Serve with cocktail sauce. Serves 4.

Stephanie's Fireside Asparagus

Laura Hill
Gladewater, TX

Every year we camp with a group of our friends in the Piney Woods of east Texas. My girlfriend Stephanie makes this little treat for a pre-meal snack. It has become a tradition...even the kids look forward to it!

2 1-lb. bunches asparagus,
   trimmed
1/2 c. butter, thinly sliced

1/2 t. chili powder
salt and pepper to taste

Lay asparagus in a single layer on a large piece of aluminum foil; slightly roll up edges of foil about 1/2 inch. Lay butter evenly over asparagus; sprinkle with seasonings. Place foil onto the flames of the campfire or fire pit. As butter melts, use tongs to turn spears slightly; cook until tender. Move foil off the flame to the edge of the fire pit to keep warm. Remove with tongs to serve. Serves 8.

Mississippi Hushpuppies

Judy Scherer
Benton, MO

My dad loved to go fishing. He would make these hushpuppies almost every week when I was growing up. We like them with mustard for dipping.

3/4 c. self-rising cornmeal
1/2 c. self-rising flour
1-1/2 T. baking powder
3 eggs, beaten
1/2 c. onion, diced
1/4 c. buttermilk
oil or bacon drippings for deep frying

In a bowl, combine cornmeal, flour, baking powder, eggs and onion. Stir in enough buttermilk to moisten mixture; stir until well mixed. Heat several inches of oil or drippings in a cast-iron skillet over medium-high heat. Drop batter into hot oil by teaspoonfuls. Fry until golden on both sides. Drain; serve warm. Makes 2 dozen.

On the way to your campsite, if you see a sign for a tag or barn sale, don't pass it by! You're sure to find oodles of ideas for bringing whimsy to your garden back home. Plant herbs or flowers in a pair of cast-off garden boots, washstands, wheelbarrows or leaky watering cans.

Fried Cabbage & Taters

Sharon Beverley-Beel
Freeport, IL

A simple recipe anyone can make. It even tastes great reheated!

1 head cabbage, coarsely
  chopped
1 onion, diced
2 t. oil

6 potatoes, peeled and diced
1 lb. Kielbasa sausage, diced
salt and pepper

In a large skillet over medium heat, cook cabbage and onion in oil until cabbage starts to wilt, about 5 minutes. Add potatoes and Kielbasa; season with salt and pepper. Cook until potatoes are tender, stirring occasionally, about 15 minutes. Serves 4 to 6.

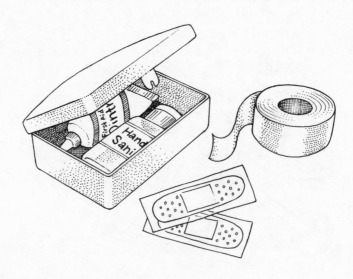

Be prepared with a handy little travel first-aid kit! Pack a plastic travel soap dish with adhesive bandages, antiseptic wipes, gauze pads, tweezers, cotton swabs, a tiny bottle of hand sanitizer and any other items your family might need. You'll be glad you did!

Grandma's Skillet Tomatoes

Marcia Shaffer
Conneaut Lake, PA

This recipe is so easy and it's always a hit with the guys!

1/4 c. milk
1/2 c. seasoned dry bread
   crumbs
1 T. green onion, minced
1 T. grated Parmesan cheese
1 t. Italian seasoning

1 t. salt
6 tomatoes, sliced 1/2-inch thick
2 T. olive oil
1/2 c. shredded mozzarella
   cheese

Place milk in a shallow bowl. In a separate bowl, combine bread crumbs, onion, Parmesan cheese and seasonings; mix well. Dip tomatoes into milk; coat with crumb mixture. Heat oil in a cast-iron skillet over medium-high heat. Cook tomatoes, a few at a time, until golden, about 2 minutes per side. Remove to a plate; sprinkle with mozzarella cheese. Serves 6.

Crispy Zucchini & Onion

Jenita Davison
La Plata, MO

This is my husband's favorite way to use all the zucchini from our garden. It's spicy and crisp...just the way we like it!

1 egg
2 to 3 T. evaporated milk
1/4 c. cornmeal
1/2 c. all-purpose flour
1 t. seasoned salt

1/2 t. garlic salt
1 t. pepper
1 to 2 zucchini, thinly sliced
3 to 4 T. oil
1 onion, thinly sliced

In a shallow bowl, beat egg and milk. Combine dry ingredients in a large plastic zipping bag. Add zucchini to egg mixture; stir to coat. Add zucchini to bag; shake well to coat. Heat oil in a cast-iron skillet over medium-high heat. Cook zucchini until crisp on one side. Coat onion in egg and cornmeal mixtures; add to skillet. Continue cooking until tender and crisp on both sides. Serves 4.

Chuck Wagon Beans

Paulette Alexander
Newfoundland, Canada

This recipe is terrific if you need a dish for a potluck...it makes enough for a crowd! It also freezes wonderfully for those evenings when you just don't feel like cooking.

1-1/2 lbs. ground beef
1 lb. bacon, diced
2 onions, diced
6 to 7 15-oz. cans baked beans
   with molasses
1-1/4 c. catsup

1-1/3 c. boiling water
3 T. mustard
2 cubes beef bouillon
2 cloves garlic, minced
1/4 to 1/2 c. brown sugar,
   to taste

In a large Dutch oven over medium heat, brown beef, bacon and onions; drain. Stir in remaining ingredients, adding brown sugar a little at a time to desired sweetness. Cover and simmer over low heat for 90 minutes to 2 hours, stirring occasionally. Makes 8 to 10 servings.

Host a backyard bonfire weenie roast in the fall when the weather turns cool and crisp. Serve up hearty Chuck Wagon Beans and simmering spiced cider. Sure to warm hearts as well as hands!

One-Pot Cheesy Spaghetti

Kristie Rigo
Friedens, PA

My husband likes this hearty dish better than traditional spaghetti. And there's just one pot to clean...how easy is that?

1 lb. ground beef or turkey
1 onion, chopped
1 green pepper, chopped
28-oz. can stewed or diced
   tomatoes
4-oz. can sliced mushrooms,
   drained

1 c. water
2 t. sugar
1 to 2 t. chili powder
1 t. salt
8-oz. pkg. spaghetti, broken up
1 c. shredded Cheddar cheese

In a Dutch oven over medium heat, brown meat with onion and green pepper; drain. Add tomatoes with juice, mushrooms, water, sugar and seasonings; bring to a simmer. Stir in spaghetti. Cook, stirring occasionally, for about 30 minutes, until spaghetti is tender. Add a little more water if needed. Remove from heat; sprinkle with cheese. Cover and let stand until cheese is melted. Serves 4.

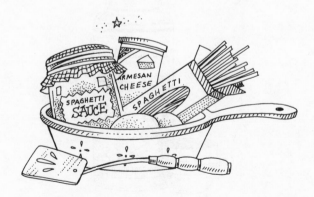

Camp cooking is super-easy when you chop or shred veggies and cheese at home, then pack in plastic zipping bags and place in a cooler. Don't chop potatoes or apples ahead of time, though, as they'll darken before being cooked.

Trailblazer Spuds

Mary Lou Thomas
Portland, ME

We camp often and really enjoy this simple meal of potatoes baked in the coals.

4 russet potatoes
1/2 lb. ground beef
1 c. shredded Cheddar cheese
1/2 c. salsa

Garnish: sour cream, sliced
green onions, chopped
black olives

Wrap each potato in heavy-duty aluminum foil. Pierce potatoes several times with a fork through the foil. Place potatoes in hot campfire coals. Cook for about one hour, turning frequently, until tender. Shortly before serving time, brown beef in a small skillet. Drain; stir in salsa and cheese. Unwrap potatoes; slice open. Top with beef mixture and desired garnishes. Serves 4.

On chilly evenings, welcome campers with a warming beverage...great for a tailgating thermos too. In a kettle, combine a 48-ounce bottle of vegetable cocktail juice with four cans of beef broth. (Choose low-sodium versions if you like.) Simmer until heated through and serve in big mugs.

GATHER 'ROUND THE CAMPFIRE

Hobo Stew

Lori Bryan
Huntsville, AR

Very fun and easy to do for a bonfire get-together. Ask each person to bring along a can of veggies to add to the pot...every time you make it, it will be different!

1 to 1-1/2 lbs. ground beef
salt, pepper and other
   seasonings to taste
16-oz. bottle tomato juice
Optional: 16-oz. can kidney
   beans, drained

3 to 4 16-oz. cans mixed
   vegetables, hominy or other
   veggies, drained
1/2 to 1 c. beef broth or water

Brown beef in a large Dutch oven over medium heat. Drain; stir in seasonings. Add tomato juice, vegetables and enough broth or water to cover. Bring to a boil; reduce heat to low. Cover and simmer until heated through, about 20 to 30 minutes. Serves 6 to 8.

All-in-One Pierogie Skillet

Linda Belon
Wintersville, OH

A delicious one-dish dinner...very welcome after a big day of hiking, bicycling or swimming!

1 lb. ground beef
1 T. oil
16-oz. pkg. frozen pierogies,
   thawed
1/2 t. salt

1/4 t. pepper
10-oz. pkg. frozen broccoli
   flowerets, thawed
1 c. shredded Cheddar cheese

In a large skillet, brown beef in oil for 5 minutes. Drain; add pierogies and cook for 4 to 5 minutes, until heated through. Stir in salt, pepper and broccoli; top with cheese. Reduce heat to low. Cover and cook for 4 to 5 minutes, until broccoli is heated through and cheese is melted. Serves 4.

Keep a box of baking soda on hand at your campsite...
it's an excellent fire extinguisher.

Tina's Quick-Fix BBQ

Tina George
El Dorado, AR

One night when we needed a quick meal I came up with this recipe. My family loves anything barbecued, so this was a real winner with them! Serve it as the main dish, sprinkled with shredded Cheddar cheese, or spoon into a bun for a quick BBQ sandwich.

1 T. oil
3 boneless, skinless chicken
   breasts, cut into 1-1/2 inch
   cubes

1 c. onion, chopped
1/2 lb. smoked pork sausage,
   sliced 1-inch thick
1 c. favorite barbecue sauce

Heat oil in a large skillet over medium heat. Add chicken and onion. Cook, stirring often, until chicken is just slightly pink in the center. Add sausage to skillet. Cook until chicken is no longer pink in the center and onion is transparent. Add barbecue sauce; stir until mixture is coated. Cover and simmer over low heat for 15 minutes. Serves 4.

Try packing pita bread, flatbread or tortillas for camping instead of regular loaf bread. They're tasty warmed up on a griddle over the fire and won't crush when packed.

GATHER 'ROUND THE CAMPFIRE

Grilled Pizza Wraps

Kathy Tormaschy
Richardton, ND

A quick, easy and very good snack or even a meal. I've substituted different cheeses and have used ham in place of the pepperoni... the wraps always turn out delicious!

4 8-inch flour tortillas
1 T. margarine, softened
1/4 c. pizza sauce

2 c. shredded Cheddar cheese
1/2 c. sliced pepperoni

Heat a skillet over medium heat. Spread one side of a tortilla with margarine. Add tortilla to skillet, margarine-side down. Spoon one tablespoon pizza sauce on half of the tortilla; top with 1/2 cup cheese and several pepperoni slices. Fold over; cook until golden on both sides. Repeat with remaining ingredients. Serves 4.

Hot Sausage Dip

Laura Aivaz
Plainville, IN

When my sister-in-law and I first tried this dip, we could not stop eating it! It has become a family favorite for any kind of party.

16-oz. pkg. hot or mild ground
  pork sausage
15-oz. can diced tomatoes with
  green chiles, drained

2 8-oz. pkgs. cream cheese,
  softened
corn or tortilla chips

Brown sausage in a large skillet over medium heat; drain. Add tomatoes; heat through. Add cream cheese; simmer until melted and stir well. Keep warm in skillet over low heat. Serve with corn or tortilla chips. Serves 12.

Ten-Can Soup

Jill Steeley
Broken Arrow, OK

After enjoying a delicious soup at a local restaurant, I concocted this recipe to recapture the experience. For a hotter version, stir in a can of tomatoes with chiles and a teaspoon of chili powder.

2 14-oz. cans chicken broth
10-3/4 oz. can cream of celery
   soup
2 10-oz. cans chicken
16-oz. can red beans, drained
   and rinsed
16-oz. can white beans, drained
   and rinsed

16-oz. can pinto beans, drained
   and rinsed
15-oz. can Italian-seasoned
   diced tomatoes
15-oz. can sliced carrots
saltine crackers

Pour chicken broth into a large Dutch oven over medium heat. Whisk in celery soup. Break up chicken with a fork; add chicken and its liquid to the pan. Add beans and undrained tomatoes and carrots; stir well. Cover and simmer until heated through, about 20 minutes. Serve with crackers. Makes 8 servings.

Pop up some campfire popcorn! Top an 18-inch square of heavy-duty aluminum foil with 2 tablespoons popping corn and 2 tablespoons oil. Fold ends to close, forming a loose pouch. Attach a long stick and hold the pouch over hot coals. When popcorn begins to pop, start shaking the pouch. When the popping stops, remove from heat. Open carefully. Top with butter and salt...share with four friends!

Herbed Corn on the Cob

Jen Stout
Blandon, PA

Fresh corn and fresh thyme are delicious together.

4 to 6 ears corn in husks
2 T. butter, melted
2 t. lemon juice

1 t. fresh thyme, snipped
salt and pepper to taste

Peel corn husks back but do not remove; remove silk. Cover corn with cold water; soak at least one hour. Drain well. Press husks back into place, tying tips of husks together with moistened kitchen string if desired. Grill corn over medium heat for about 25 minutes, until tender, turning several times. Carefully remove husks and string. Combine remaining ingredients in a small bowl; brush over corn just before serving. Serves 4 to 6.

Mini Parmesan Corn Cobs

Krista Marshall
Fort Wayne, IN

We love our summer pool parties, and it's always fun to plan the food. Mini ears of corn are much easier to handle!

3 ears corn, husked and broken
   in half
1/4 c. grated Parmesan cheese

4 t. dried parsley
salt to taste
6 T. butter, melted

Bring a large pot of water to a boil over high heat. Add corn and cook until tender, about 6 minutes. Drain well. Combine cheese, parsley and salt in a cup; mix well. Use a pastry brush to coat hot corn with butter; sprinkle with cheese mixture. Let stand about one minute before serving, so cheese mixture sticks. Makes 6 servings.

Sing songs around the campfire. Who cares if someone's off-key?
It's a fun way to make the best memories!

Summertime Goulash

Cindy McKinnon
El Dorado, AR

I was over at my friend Lea Ann's one summer day. She had this simmering on the stove and it smelled sooo good! It is the best if you have fresh vegetables, but it's even good with frozen veggies.

2-3 T. bacon drippings or oil
6 to 8 redskin potatoes, peeled
   and cubed
1 onion, chopped

8 to 10 okra, chopped
seasoned salt or salt to taste
pepper to taste

Heat drippings or oil in a large cast-iron skillet over medium-high. Add potatoes, onion and okra. Season with salt and pepper. Cook for 5 minutes; stir. Reduce heat to medium-low. Cover and cook about 20 minutes, stirring often, until potatoes are tender. Serves 8.

Skillet New Potatoes

Regina Ferrigno
Gooseberry Patch

Yum! You don't even need to peel the potatoes.

2 T. butter
2 T. oil
2 lbs. new potatoes

2 to 3 cloves garlic
salt and pepper to taste

Combine all ingredients in a Dutch oven. Cover and cook over low heat for 40 to 60 minutes, shaking covered pan occasionally, until potatoes are golden and tender. Season with additional salt and pepper, if desired. Serves 4.

Ripe tomatoes are such a treat! Pick up a basket at a roadstand on the way to camp. Serve simply with a dash of oil & vinegar, a pinch of salt and a toss of chopped fresh basil.

Fry Dough or Bannock

LeeAnn Bird
Saskatchewan, Canada

Bannock was brought to North America from Europe, then became a tradition made by Native Americans and Native Canadians. Most natives remember their grandparents' good bannock. I remember my mom making it often. When I visit friends in different First Nations communities around Saskatchewan, it seems every home has one or two loaves made fresh everyday.

2 c. all-purpose flour
2 T. baking powder
1/4 t. salt
Optional: 1/4 c. oil

1/2 c. milk
1/2 c. warm water
Optional: oil for deep frying
Garnish: berry jam

In a bowl, mix together flour, baking powder and salt. Make a well in flour mixture. Pour in milk, water and oil; stir well. Turn dough out onto a floured surface; knead lightly for 2 minutes. For Bannock, form into a flat loaf or cut into biscuit-size pieces; place on a lightly greased baking sheet. Bake at 375 degrees for 10 to 20 minutes, until lightly golden. For Fry Dough, omit the 1/4 cup oil. Roll out dough; cut into several hand-size pieces. Heat several inches oil in a cast-iron skillet over medium-high heat. Fry dough, a few pieces at a time, for about 2 minutes per side, until golden. Drain. Serve warm, topped with jam if desired. Makes 4 to 6 servings.

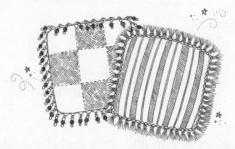

Whip up a stack of comfy sit-upons. Cut a 30-inch by 15-inch rectangle of colorful vinyl...dollar-store tablecloths are perfect. Fold in half and punch holes around the three cut sides. Stitch two sides with yarn and a big needle; tuck in a big foam square. Stitch the last side and slip-stitch the opening closed.

Dawn's Pie-Iron Pizzas

Dawn Henning
Gooseberry Patch

This is my favorite campfire meal. Growing up, my family did a lot of camping and we always made these pizzas. Even today we have them whenever we have a fire at a campground or in the backyard.

1 loaf sliced bread
1/2 c. butter, softened
1 to 2 15-oz. jars pizza sauce
8-oz. pkg. pepperoni slices
1 onion, diced
1 green pepper, diced
8-oz. jar sliced mushrooms, drained
4-oz. jar sliced black olives, drained
8-oz. pkg. shredded mozzarella cheese

Preheat pie iron in campfire. Spread 2 slices bread with butter on one side. Place one slice, butter-side down, on hotter side of pie iron. Spoon desired amount of pizza sauce over both slices of bread. Top one slice with pepperoni, vegetables, a handful of cheese and remaining bread slice. Close pie iron. Cook over campfire for several minutes; opening carefully to check how toasted the bread is. Close pie iron; flip over and cook other side to desired doneness. Makes 6 to 8 servings.

Campfire Corn Dogs

Jamie Johnson
Gooseberry Patch

Our favorite county fair treat!

8-1/2 oz. pkg. corn muffin mix
1/3 c. milk
1 egg
8 to 10 hot dogs
Garnish: catsup, mustard

In a bowl, stir together muffin mix, milk and egg until moistened. Place 2 hot dogs inside a well-greased pie iron. Add enough batter to fill bottom of pie iron. Close pie iron; turn over and cook over campfire for 3 minutes. Turn over; cook for another 3 minutes, or until cornbread is set. Repeat with remaining ingredients. Slice between hot dogs; serve with catsup and mustard. Serves 4 to 5.

Reuben Pudgie Pies

Geneva Rogers
Gillette, WY

The first time we took our children camping, they laughed when I told them we were having pudgie pies for lunch. But they helped put the pies together and ate every bite!

1 to 2 T. butter, softened
4 slices rye bread
4 to 6 thin slices deli corned beef
2 slices Swiss cheese

1/4 c. sauerkraut, well drained
Thousand Island salad dressing
  to taste

Spread butter over one side of each bread slice. Place one slice in a pie iron, butter-side down. Top with 2 to 3 slices corned beef, a cheese slice, half of sauerkraut, salad dressing and another bread slice. Close pie iron. Cook over campfire, turning until both sides of bread are golden. Repeat to make a second sandwich. Serves 2.

Tuna Melt Toasties

Darrell Lawry
Kissimmee, FL

This is my favorite campfire meal!

2 2-1/2 oz. pouches tuna,
  drained
1 to 2 t. pickle relish, drained
1 to 2 T. mayonnaise

4 slices bread
1 to 2 T. butter, softened
2 slices Cheddar or Swiss cheese
2 slices ripe tomato

In a bowl, mix tuna, relish and mayonnaise. Spread butter on one side of each bread slice. Place one slice in a pie iron, butter-side down. Top with half of tuna mixture, one cheese slice, one tomato slice and another bread slice. Close pie iron. Cook on both sides over campfire until toasty and golden. Repeat to make a second sandwich. Makes 2 servings.

Buffalo Chicken Pizza Pockets

Patty Bowen
Westfield, NY

This recipe came about from my love of camping and campfire cooking, not to mention chicken pizza! Replace the hot sauce with BBQ sauce to make BBQ chicken pizza pockets.

1 lb. boneless chicken, grilled
   and diced
cayenne hot pepper sauce
   to taste
1 loaf sliced Italian bread

1/2 c. butter, softened
1/2 c. ranch salad dressing
8-oz. pkg. shredded pizza-blend
   cheese

In a bowl, combine chicken and enough hot sauce to coat well; set aside. For each sandwich, spray a pie iron generously with non-stick vegetable spray. Butter 2 slices of bread and place butter-side down in pie iron. Spread one slice with one tablespoon salad dressing; top with 1/4 cup cheese and 1/4 cup chicken mixture. Close pie iron. Toast in coals until golden on both sides. Repeat with remaining ingredients. Makes 6 to 8 servings.

The fire is the main comfort of the camp...it is as well
for cheerfulness as for warmth and dryness.
– Henry David Thoreau

FOIL PACKET DINNERS

Kiddies' Chicken Packets

Dawn Smith
Cape Girardeau, MO

I teach a children's cooking class, and for the finale the students prepare this recipe for their parents. These packets turn out perfectly every time, and the chicken is so tender and yummy! The parents are always so impressed. Serve right from the packet, if you like.

1 c. Italian salad dressing,
    divided
4 boneless, skinless chicken
    breasts
salt and pepper to taste

3 potatoes, thinly sliced
10 baby carrots, sliced
1 stalk celery, chopped
1 onion, sliced

Drizzle four 18-inch lengths of heavy-duty aluminum foil with one tablespoon salad dressing each. Season chicken breasts with salt and pepper. Layer each piece of foil with one chicken breast, one tablespoon salad dressing, potatoes divided between packets, one tablespoon salad dressing and remaining vegetables divided between packets. Drizzle with remaining salad dressing. Fold foil together to make packets; seal tightly but allow a little room at the top. Grill over medium-low heat for 45 minutes, until chicken juices run clear when pierced. Packets may also be baked on baking sheets at 350 degrees for 45 minutes. Makes 4 servings.

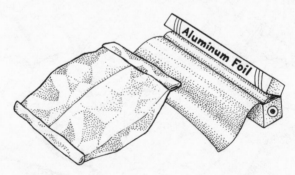

Heavy-duty aluminum foil is best for making grilling packets. To form a packet, bring up the sides and double-fold across the top, then crimp the ends closed. Leave a little extra space for heat to circulate inside. After cooking, watch out for escaping hot steam when you open the package.

Enchilada-Stuffed Poblanos

Carolyn Deckard
Bedford, IN

My son-in-laws love this spicy recipe! We make them on the grill when camping, and bake in the oven for our family cookouts. Either way, it's a winner.

2-1/2 c. cooked chicken, shredded
15-oz. can black beans, drained and rinsed
11-oz. can corn, drained
10-oz. can diced tomatoes and green chiles, drained

10-oz. can enchilada sauce
2 c. shredded Mexican-blend cheese, divided
1 t. salt
6 poblano peppers, halved lengthwise and seeded

In a large bowl, combine chicken, beans, corn, tomatoes, enchilada sauce, 1-1/2 cups cheese and salt. Fill pepper halves evenly with chicken mixture. Wrap each half loosely in aluminum foil. Grill over medium-high heat for about 20 minutes, until heated through and peppers are tender. Unwrap; sprinkle with remaining cheese and let stand several minutes, until cheese is melted. Unwrapped peppers may also be placed cut-side up in 2 lightly greased 13"x9" baking pans. Bake, uncovered, at 350 degrees for 30 minutes; sprinkle with remaining cheese. Return to oven for 5 minutes, or until cheese is melted. Makes 12 servings.

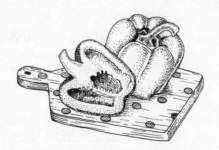

Grill your own roasted sweet peppers. Slice lengthwise into quarters and remove the seeds. Place the peppers directly on a hot grill. Cook until charred. Use tongs to drop peppers into a plastic zipping bag; cool. The skins will pull right off! Use right away or freeze for later use.

Vagabond Chicken Bundles

*Janice Marshall
Tucson, AZ*

I used to love hobo hamburger packs when I was a Girl Scout and went camping. Then I figured out this version with chicken and squash...it's perfect for summertime meals.

1 T. olive oil
3 c. zucchini, sliced
3 c. yellow squash, sliced
6 boneless, skinless chicken
    breasts

2 c. shredded mozzarella cheese
Italian seasoning and pepper
    to taste

Brush six 10-inch lengths of heavy-duty aluminum foil with olive oil. Top each square with 1/2 cup zucchini and and 1/2 cup squash. Cut several slits in each chicken breast with a knife tip; lay on top of squash. Sprinkle with seasonings. Top chicken evenly with cheese. Wrap bundles lightly in foil. Grill over medium-high heat for 30 minutes, or until chicken juices run clear. Serves 6.

Sweet-and-Sour Chicken

*Cindy Neel
Gooseberry Patch*

Serve over hot rice and top with chow mein noodles.

4 boneless, skinless chicken
    breasts or thighs
1 c. sweet-and-sour sauce,
    divided

8-oz. can pineapple chunks,
    drained
1 green pepper, thinly sliced
1/4 onion, thinly sliced

On each of four 18-inch lengths of heavy-duty aluminum foil, place one chicken piece, one tablespoon sauce and 1/4 each of pineapple, pepper and onion. Drizzle with remaining sauce. Fold over foil; seal edges to make a packet. Grill, covered, over medium heat for 15 to 20 minutes, until chicken juices run clear. May also bake packets on baking sheets at 350 degrees for 35 to 45 minutes. Serves 4.

Italian Chicken in Foil

Ellie Brandel
Milwaukie, OR

So easy to put together...let each camper make his or her own.

1 boneless, skinless chicken
   breast or thigh
1 potato, peeled and
   cut lengthwise into
   1/8-inch slices
1 zucchini, sliced 1/4-inch thick

salt to taste
3 black olives
2 t. tomato sauce
1/2 t. dried oregano
1 t. butter, diced

Season chicken, potato and zucchini with salt; set aside. Layer potato and zucchini slices on an 18-inch length of heavy-duty aluminum foil. Top with chicken, olives, tomato sauce and oregano; dot with butter. Wrap securely in foil. Grill packet over medium heat for 25 to 30 minutes on each side, or until chicken juices run clear and vegetables are tender. Makes one serving.

Serve up frosty lemonade or herbal ice tea with blueberry skewers.
Simply slide blueberries onto a wooden skewer until covered.
Top with a fresh mint leaf...easy!

Georgia Peach Smoked Chops

Staci Prickett
Montezuma, GA

*This recipe only has two ingredients, but it's a real tummy-pleaser!
A great recipe for that next camping trip.*

6 to 8 smoked pork chops   16-oz. jar peach preserves

Grill pork chops over medium-high heat for 4 to 5 minutes on each
side, just until browned. Place chops on a 24-inch length of heavy-
duty aluminum foil. Spoon preserves over chops. Wrap in foil, forming
a packet. Grill for another 10 to 15 minutes, until chops are heated
through and glazed. Makes 6 to 8 servings.

Pork Chop Bundles

Karen Overholt
Kennewick, WA

*When my kids were home, we always had fun fixing dinner
together and coming up with different ideas. This tasty recipe
is my son Cory's creation.*

1 bone-in pork chop,   1/2 onion, thinly sliced
   1/2-inch thick   1 fresh or frozen ear corn on the
salt and pepper to taste   cob, husks and silk removed
1/2 t. oil   Optional: 2 to 3 ice cubes
1 potato, thinly sliced

Season pork chop with salt and pepper. Heat oil in a skillet over
medium-high heat; brown chop on both sides. Layer chop and
remaining ingredients on a 14-inch length of heavy-duty aluminum
foil in order listed, seasoning with more salt and pepper. Add ice cubes,
if fresh corn is used. Wrap securely. Cover and grill over medium-high
heat for about one hour. May also bake on a baking sheet at 350
degrees for one hour. Serves one.

FOIL PACKET
DINNERS

Barbecue Spareribs

Patty Strock
Liberty Center, OH

The only way to describe these ribs is "finger-lickin' good!"

2-1/2 to 3 lbs. pork spareribs,
    cut into serving-size pieces
seasoned salt and pepper
    to taste

1-1/2 c. favorite barbecue sauce
1 T. all-purpose flour

Place a large aluminum foil grilling bag in a shallow baking pan. Spray inside of bag with non-stick vegetable spray. Season ribs with salt and pepper; arrange in bag in an even layer. Combine barbecue sauce and flour in a bowl; spread evenly over ribs. Double-fold end of bag to seal. Slide bag onto grill over medium heat. Cover and cook for one hour. Carefully cut bag open and fold top back, to allow steam to escape. Remove ribs to grill and continue grilling for 15 minutes, or until ribs are browned on both sides. Makes 4 servings.

A condiment basket filled with jars of relish, pickles, barbecue sauce, mustard and catsup is a great gift for anyone who loves to grill. Tuck in a set of tongs, an apron and a favorite grilling cookbook...so thoughtful!

Picnic in a Pan

Linda Williamson
Bluefield, WV

*Like a summer fellowship picnic in a dish! Feel free
to add other favorite veggies too.*

4 potatoes, peeled and cubed
4 ears sweet corn, broken in half
4 tomatoes, sliced
4 green peppers, sliced
1/2 lb. mushrooms, trimmed
and halved

1 lb. smoked pork sausage,
quartered
1/2 c. butter, sliced
1/2 c. water
1/2 c. Worcestershire sauce
seasoned salt to taste

Layer vegetables and sausage on 24-inch length of heavy-duty
aluminum foil. Dot with butter. Drizzle with water and Worcestershire
sauce. Add seasoned salt to taste. Fold up sides of foil; seal into a
packet. Grill over medium heat for about one hour, until vegetables are
tender. Ingredients may also be layered in a deep 13"x9" baking pan.
Cover with aluminum foil; bake at 375 degrees for about one hour.
Serves 4.

Vintage tin picnic baskets are terrific...so roomy, they easily tote
goodies to & from a picnic, wipe clean in a jiffy and can be found in
a variety of colors and fun patterns.

FOIL PACKET
DINNERS

Best Potato & Bacon Dish

Lynn Colley
Barling, AR

*Our children loved this recipe and considered it a special dinner.
Recently, I prepared this dish for friends...the guys wanted
to hug the cook!*

4 baking potatoes, quartered
1 sweet or white onion, thinly
   sliced and separated
   into rings
4 slices bacon, crisply cooked
   and crumbled

8-oz. pkg. American cheese
   slices
6 T. butter, sliced

Place potatoes on an 18-inch length of heavy-duty aluminum foil.
Layer with onion rings, crumbled bacon and cheese slices; dot with
butter. Fold over sides and ends of foil, forming a packet. Grill over
medium-high for about one hour, until potatoes are tender. Ingredients
may also be layered in a lightly greased 13"x9" baking pan. Cover with
aluminum foil; bake at 375 degrees for about 45 minutes. Serves 4.

Remember to tote along some blankets or folding stools when you
go camping...there's nothing like sitting around a glowing campfire
stargazing, swapping stories and just savoring time
together with family & friends!

Ham & Potato Pockets

Trisha Cooper
Spanish Fork, UT

I made these pockets for my family on a camping trip...my husband and all five children loved them! They've become a camping tradition we look forward to. Precooking the potatoes cuts the grilling time in half.

1 c. potato, peeled, diced and
    partially cooked
1 c. cooked ham, diced
1/2 onion, sliced and separated
    into rings

salt and pepper to taste
2 to 3 T. butter
1 c. shredded Monterey Jack
    cheese

On an 18-inch length of heavy-duty aluminum foil, layer potato, ham and onion. Season with salt and pepper; dot with butter and sprinkle with cheese. Bring up sides of foil; fold down top 2 to 3 times and fold ends 2 to 3 times to seal packet. Grill over medium heat for about 20 minutes, until heated through and cheese is melted. Packet may also be placed on a baking sheet; bake at 350 degrees for about 20 minutes. Makes one to two servings.

Watch for meteor showers. The best time is August 10th to 13th, called the Perseids, when you can see an average of 65 meteors light up the sky each hour...it's almost like enjoying fireworks!

FOIL PACKET
DINNERS

Beefy Stew Packets

Zoe Bennett
Columbia, SC

Mmm...this savory beef stew makes its own tasty gravy, and there's no pot to clean afterwards! Add some fluffy biscuits for a really satisfying dinner.

2 lbs. beef chuck roast, cubed
6 potatoes, peeled and diced
6 carrots, peeled and thinly
   sliced
8-oz. pkg. sliced mushrooms
6 T. onion, chopped
Optional: 3 stalks celery, sliced

2 10-3/4 oz. cans golden
   mushroom soup
1/2 c. fresh parsley, chopped
salt and pepper to taste
6 T. water
hot pepper sauce to taste

Divide all ingredients among six 18-inch lengths of heavy-duty aluminum foil. Bring up sides of foil to make packets; seal ends. Grill over medium heat for about one hour, until beef and vegetables are tender. Makes 6 servings.

New plastic pails make colorful, unbreakable picnic servers for chips and snacks. Afterward, the kids can use them for treasure hunting around the picnic grounds, beach or backyard.

Stuffed Pepper Slices

Judy Murphy
Sparland, IL

In the summer, we love stuffed bell peppers when the peppers are fresh from the garden, but I hate to heat up the kitchen and want simple quick meals. So I tried this recipe...it's wonderful!

3 to 4 green or red peppers
1 lb. lean ground beef
2/3 c. plain dry bread crumbs
1 egg, beaten
1/4 c. milk

1 T. onion, minced
1/2 t. salt or salt substitute
1/4 t. pepper
1/2 t. Worcestershire sauce

Slice peppers crosswise into 2-inch rings. Cut the leftover bottoms and tops into one-inch strips. Place pepper rings on heavy-duty aluminum foil sprayed with non-stick vegetable spray. Mix together remaining ingredients. Spoon beef mixture evenly into pepper rings. Place foil with pepper rings on a preheated grill over medium-high heat. Arrange remaining pepper slices on foil around pepper rings. Grill for 4 minutes. Carefully turn over pepper rings; top with Sauce. Grill an additional 4 minutes, or until beef and peppers are cooked to desired doneness. Makes 4 to 6 servings.

Sauce:

1/4 c. catsup
2 T. brown sugar, packed

1/2 t. dry mustard
1/4 t. nutmeg

Mix all ingredients in a small bowl.

Dining outdoors on a hot, humid day? Keep salt free-flowing by placing a few dry grains of rice in the shaker.

Angie's Hobo Dinner

*Angie Venable
Ostrander, OH*

We love these hobo dinner packets. They are fun to make as a family, with everyone helping while we go over our days together. Some of us like onions and mushrooms and some don't...but each of us has something we like in them!

1-1/2 lbs. ground beef
1 to 2 T. Worcestershire sauce
1/2 t. seasoned pepper
1/2 t. dried basil
1/8 t. garlic powder
4 redskin potatoes, sliced

4 carrots, peeled and halved
1 c. sliced mushrooms
1 onion, sliced
olive oil to taste
dried parsley to taste

In a bowl, combine beef, Worcestershire sauce and seasonings. Mix well and form into 4 to 6 patties. Place each patty on an 18-inch length of heavy-duty aluminum foil. Top patties evenly with vegetables. Drizzle with olive oil; sprinkle with parsley. Seal foil packets. Grill packets over medium heat, or cook on hot campfire coals, for 15 to 20 minutes per side. May also place packets on baking sheets; bake at 375 degrees for about one hour. Serves 4 to 6.

Make tonight a family game night...invite all the other campers too! Bring along all your favorite board games and play to your heart's content. Small prizes for winners and foil bowls of campfire popcorn are a must!

Bountiful Hobo Packs

Lynda Bolton
East Peoria, IL

My dad owned 17 acres in southern Illinois, and every summer we sold our home-grown vegetables. My stepmom made this recipe often with our abundant produce. After I had my own family, the four of us would make this favorite meal often, using fresh veggies from our local farmers' market. It's great to take to potlucks as well!

2 lbs. ground beef
1 onion, diced
1 green pepper, cubed
2 potatoes, peeled and sliced
1 bunch broccoli, cut into
    bite-size flowerets
8 carrots, sliced, or
    1 lb. baby carrots
1 to 2 zucchini, sliced

3 ears sweet corn, husked and
    each broken into 3 pieces
1 head cabbage, cut into chunks
5 tomatoes, cubed
1 t. seasoned salt
1/2 t. pepper
Optional: 1/2 t. garlic powder
1/2 c. butter, sliced

Spray eight 18-inch lengths of heavy-duty aluminum foil or a large disposable aluminum baking pan with non-stick vegetable spray. Break up uncooked beef; divide among foil pieces or place in pan. Layer with vegetables. Add seasonings to taste; top with pats of butter. Wrap tightly if making individual packs, or cover pan tightly with aluminum foil. Grill over medium heat, or bake at 350 degrees, for 1-1/2 hours. Serves 8.

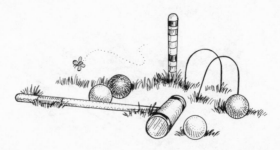

Take the family out to dinner...at a nearby park! While a simple meal cooks on the grill, everyone can swing on the swings, play croquet or just enjoy the sights and sounds of nature. Afterwards, make homemade ice cream or s'mores for dessert...what fun!

Barbecued Pot Roast

Patricia Lisby
Greenwood, IN

My kids used to ask me to make this delicious,
tender roast every week...it's a real family favorite!

4-1/2 to 5-lb. beef chuck roast
1 T. curry powder
pepper to taste
4 T. olive oil
1 yellow onion, chopped
1 c. dry red burgundy wine
   or beef broth
1 c. catsup

1/2 c. vinegar
1/2 c. water
2 T. brown sugar, packed
2 T. Worcestershire sauce
1/2 t. dry mustard
smoke-flavored cooking sauce
   to taste
salt to taste

Rub roast with curry powder and pepper. Heat oil in a large skillet over medium-high heat. Brown roast on all sides; drain. Place roast in a large piece of aluminum foil. Meanwhile, in a saucepan, combine remaining ingredients except salt. Simmer over medium heat until onion is soft, stirring often. Ladle onion mixture over roast; fold foil over to seal well. Grill over medium heat for 2 hours, or until roast is tender. Packet may also be placed on a baking sheet and baked at 350 degrees for 2 hours. If desired, season to taste with salt at serving time. Makes 10 to 12 servings.

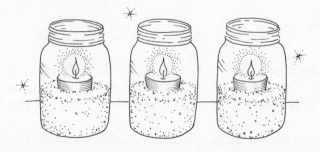

Need a quick table decoration? Fill Mason jars with coarse salt, then tuck in a votive. The salt crystals will sparkle in the flickering light...perfect for casual suppers.

Parmesan Baked Fish

Samantha Starks
Madison, WI

When I was growing up, we camped at the lake every summer. Dad always promised to catch enough fish for our dinner...but Mom always had some fish fillets tucked in the cooler just in case!

1 lb. tilapia or whitefish fillets
1/4 c. mayonnaise
1/4 c. grated Parmesan cheese

cayenne pepper to taste
2 zucchini, sliced
1/2 red pepper, thinly sliced

Place each fish fillet on an 18-inch length of heavy-duty aluminum foil. Spread with mayonnaise; sprinkle with cheese and cayenne pepper. Top with vegetables. Fold up sides to make a packet; seal well. Grill, covered, over medium-high heat for 10 to 12 minutes, or bake on baking sheets at 450 degrees for 18 to 22 minutes, until fish flakes easily with a fork. Serves 4.

Stuffed Catfish

Beth Kramer
Port Saint Lucie, FL

Toss in some veggies for a complete meal.

6-oz. pkg. cornbread
  stuffing mix
1-1/4 c. boiling water

8 2 to 3-oz. fillets catfish
salt and pepper to taste
Optional: 1/3 c. chopped pecans

In a bowl, stir together stuffing mix and water; set aside. Center one catfish fillet on each of four 18-inch lengths of heavy-duty aluminum foil. Spoon 1/4 of stuffing mixture evenly over each fillet; top with another fillet. Sprinkle with salt, pepper and pecans, if using. Form into packets. Cover and grill over medium-high heat for 8 to 10 minutes, until fish flakes easily. Makes 4 servings.

Pork & Peach Kabobs, page 55

Haddock & Creamy Dill Sauce, page 24

Black Bean Turkey Burgers, page 53

Pan-Fried Corn Fritters, page 76

Enchilada-Stuffed Pablanos, page 105

Picnic in a Pan, page 110

Zesty Beef Fajitas, page 20

Tina's All-Star Sliders on
Cornbread Buns, page 46

Grilled Pineapple Sundaes, page 194

Grilled Bacon Corn on the Cob, page 125

Edna's Refrigerator Pickles, page 192

Sizzling Bacon Asparagus, page 34

Mustard & Herb Strip Steak, page 21

Grilled Pepperoni Log, page 36

Hobo Stew, page 93

Zesty Marinated Garden Veggies, page 180

Hawaiian Chicken Kabobs, page 58

Grilled Peaches, page 198

Bacon-Wrapped BBQ Chicken, page 9

Angie's Hobo Dinner, page 115

Grilled Halibut & Lemon Sauce,
page 25

Grilled Parmesan Bread, page 40

Grilled Fresh Summer Pizza, page 63

FOIL PACKET
DINNERS

Smoky New Potatoes

Vickie
Gooseberry Patch

New potatoes are scrumptious prepared this way! They're especially yummy with the fresh sour cream dip.

1 lb. tiny new potatoes	1/3 c. sour cream
2 T. water	1/4 c. plain Greek yogurt
3/4 t. salt	Garnish: fresh snipped chives
1/2 t. pepper	

Arrange potatoes in a single layer on a 24-inch length of heavy-duty aluminum foil. Sprinkle with water, salt and pepper. Fold over foil to make a packet. Grill over medium heat for 25 to 35 minutes, until potatoes are tender. Blend sour cream and yogurt in a small bowl. Season potatoes with additional salt and pepper, if desired. Serve with sour cream mixture; sprinkle with chives. Serves 4.

Cheesy Grilled Eggplant

Edward Kielar
Whitehouse, OH

We love eggplant so we make this recipe on the grill all year 'round.

1 to 2 T. butter	2 tomatoes, sliced
1 eggplant, sliced 1/2-inch thick	8 slices Swiss cheese

Melt butter in a skillet over medium-high heat. Cook eggplant slices until tender and golden. Arrange eggplant on a 14-inch length of heavy-duty aluminum foil, reserving several slices for top. Layer with tomato and cheese slices; top with reserved eggplant slices. Wrap well. Grill over medium-high heat for 5 minutes, or until hot and cheese is melted. Serves 4.

When preparing foil packet dinners, add a few ice cubes to each packet for extra moistness.

Hot Parmesan Loaf

Mia Rossi
Charlotte, NC

We often cook out at a favorite park. It's so easy to wrap up this loaf and tuck it in the cooler to grill later.

1/2 c. butter, softened
1/3 c. shredded Parmesan
    cheese
1 loaf French bread, sliced
    1-inch thick

garlic powder and Italian
    seasoning to taste

Blend butter and cheese in a small bowl. Spread butter mixture over one side of each bread slice. Sprinkle with seasonings. Reassemble slices back into a loaf; wrap well in aluminum foil. Place on a grill over medium-low heat. Cover and cook for 8 to 12 minutes, turning occasionally, until toasty and butter is melted. Serve warm. Makes 14 to 16 servings.

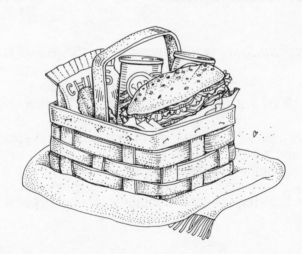

Keep a basket of picnic supplies in your car for picnics and cookouts at a moment's notice. With a quilt or tablecloth, paper napkins, plates and cups you'll always be ready to go!

Slow-Cooked Kalua Pork

Jill Ball
Highland, UT

My neighbor shared this delicious recipe with me. She lived in Hawaii for several years. No need to dig a six-foot cooking pit!

4-lb. pork butt roast
4-oz. bottle smoke-flavored
    cooking sauce, divided

kosher salt to taste
cooked rice

Place pork roast in a large slow cooker. Sprinkle sauce generously over pork, using 1/3 to 1/2 of the bottle; add salt to taste. Cover and cook on low setting for 8 hours, or on high setting for 4 hours, until very tender. Shred pork; serve over cooked rice. Serves 8.

Super-Easy BBQ Chicken

Bobbie Sofia
Lake Havasu City, AZ

I've lived in the desert Southwest most of my adult life, so I know barbecue is not just for summer! So simple to fix in your slow cooker...just add a fresh green salad for a wonderful meal.

16 chicken drumsticks and/or
    thighs, skin removed

2 c. favorite barbecue sauce
cooked rice

Place chicken in a microwave-safe dish. Cover and microwave on high for 15 minutes. Carefully remove hot chicken to a 6-quart slow cooker, spooning some barbecue sauce over each piece. Cover and cook on low setting for 6 to 8 hours. Discard bones. Serve chicken and sauce over rice. Serves 6 to 8.

Take along the slow cooker on your next RV or camping trip. Put dinner on to cook in the morning and it will practically cook itself!

Beef Dip Sandwiches

Brandie Skibinski
Salem, VA

A sure-fire hit with the whole family! The slow cooker yields really tender beef with yummy au jus sauce that's just perfect for dipping.

3 to 4-lb. beef round steak,
    chuck roast or brisket
15-oz. can beef broth
1/2 c. water
1.35-oz. pkg. onion soup mix
1-oz. pkg. au jus seasoning mix

6 to 8 sub rolls, split
6 to 8 slices mozzarella cheese
Garnish: sautéed sliced
    onions, green peppers
    and mushrooms
Optional: additional beef broth

Place beef in a large slow cooker. In a bowl, combine broth, water and mixes. Stir until combined and pour over beef. Cover and cook on low setting for 7 to 8 hours, until tender. One hour before serving, shred beef with 2 forks, or remove to a cutting board and slice thinly. Return beef to juice in slow cooker; cover and cook for final hour. For each sandwich, place several slices of beef and a slice of cheese on the bottom half of a roll. Broil just until cheese melts and roll is lightly toasted. Add desired toppings and top half of roll. Strain juice from slow cooker, adding a little more broth if needed. Serve with sandwiches for dipping. Serves 6 to 8.

Shredded beef, pork or chicken sandwiches are oh-so easy to fix
and a real crowd-pleaser! Serve them on busy family nights
or tote them to potlucks right in the slow cooker.

Sweet & Tangy BBQ Short Ribs

Kathie Cassidy
Lunenburg, MA

*Whenever I make these ribs, everyone wants seconds and
a copy of the recipe. They're so tender and yummy...
and the leftovers are just as tasty the next day.*

5 lbs. boneless beef short ribs,
    cut into serving-size portions
1-1/2 c. catsup
1/4 c. brown sugar, packed
1/4 c. red wine vinegar
3 T. honey

2 T. honey mustard
2 T. Worcestershire sauce
1 t. smoke-flavored cooking
    sauce
1/4 t. garlic powder
2 T. cornstarch

Place ribs in a large slow cooker; set aside. In a bowl, combine
remaining ingredients except cornstarch. Stir well; pour over beef.
Cover and cook on low setting for 4 hours. Sprinkle with cornstarch;
stir well. Cover and cook on low setting for one additional hour. Makes
6 to 8 servings.

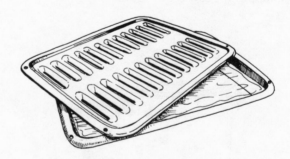

If you prefer grilled ribs, just place slow-cooked meat on
a broiler pan...pop under the broiler for a few minutes,
until it's crisp and lightly charbroiled.

Cristina's Asian Pork Ribs

Cristina Davenport
Los Alamos, NM

My husband lived in Korea for two years and he loves these Asian flavors. Whenever country-style pork ribs go on sale, I stock up on them and freeze for later use.

3 lbs. country-style pork ribs,
   cut into serving-size portions
2/3 c. soy sauce
1/2 c. water
1/4 c. rice vinegar
2 t. toasted sesame oil
2-inch piece fresh ginger, peeled
   and grated

1/2 t. garlic powder
3/4 to 1 c. brown sugar, packed
1/4 to 1/2 t. cayenne pepper
2-1/4 T. cornstarch
cooked rice
Garnish: 2 green onions, sliced
   diagonally, and 1 t. toasted
   sesame seed

Place ribs in a slow cooker; set aside. In a bowl, mix remaining ingredients except rice and garnish, adding brown sugar and cayenne pepper to taste. Pour sauce mixture over ribs. Cover and cook on low setting for 6 to 8 hours, or on high setting for 4 hours, until ribs are tender. Remove ribs to a serving platter. Strain sauce mixture and spoon over ribs. Serve ribs over hot rice, garnished as desired. Serves 6 to 8.

If it's been too long since you've visited with good friends, why not host a casual get-together? Potlucks are so easy to plan...everyone brings along their favorite dish to share. It's all about food, fun and fellowship!

Cee's Best-Ever Pulled Pork

Cecile Taylor
Fort Lauderdale, FL

My pulled pork has been requested for birthdays, showers and reunions. The ease of making it is the best part. Make sure you use Boston butt...it is the very best for pulled pork!

3 to 5-lb. Boston butt pork roast
5 to 6 onions, sliced
1-ltr. bottle root beer

2 18-oz. bottles sweet & spicy barbecue sauce

Put roast in a large slow cooker. Add onions; pour in root beer. Cover and cook on low setting for 8 hours, or until tender. Remove pork and onions from slow cooker to a large bowl. Pull roast apart with 2 forks; stir in sauce. Serves 15 to 20.

Pulled BBQ Chicken Buns

Marie Benfield
Clarkesville, GA

This is a real go-to recipe...it's so easy. Everyone I have shared it with enjoys it as much as I do. Serve with coleslaw and chips.

4 to 6 boneless, skinless chicken
   breasts
1/2 c. water
3 T. white vinegar

3 T. Worcestershire sauce
1 t. ground cumin
favorite barbecue sauce to taste
6 sandwich buns, split

In a slow cooker, combine all ingredients except barbecue sauce and buns. Cover and cook on low setting for 6 to 8 hours, until chicken is tender. Drain off liquid. Shred chicken using 2 forks. Add desired amount of sauce; cover and cook another 30 minutes. Serve chicken on buns. Makes 6 servings.

Tuck a tiny American flag toothpick in your sandwich halves! Not only fun, they're great for holding together overstuffed sandwiches.

Barbecued Beef Brisket

Marlene Swisher
Reading, KS

This slow-cooker recipe is budget-friendly and easy to prepare.

1 t. salt	1/4 t. celery seed
1 t. chili powder	1/4 t. pepper
1/2 t. garlic powder	2-1/2 lb. beef brisket, trimmed
1/4 t. onion powder	

Combine all seasonings in a small bowl; rub over brisket. Place brisket in a slow cooker. Pour half of Sauce over brisket; refrigerate remaining sauce. Cover and cook on high setting for 4 to 5 hours, until brisket is tender. Slice and serve with reserved Sauce. Makes 4 to 6 servings.

Sauce:

1/2 c. catsup	2 T. Worcestershire sauce
1/2 c. chili sauce	1 to 1-1/2 t. smoke-flavored
1/4 c. brown sugar, packed	cooking sauce
2 T. cider vinegar	1/2 t. dry mustard

Combine all ingredients in a bowl; mix well.

Fill up a relish tray with crunchy fresh cut-up veggies as a simple side dish for sandwiches. A creamy salad dressing can even do double duty as a veggie dip and a sandwich spread.

Camp-Out Chili Dogs

Kathy Grashoff
Fort Wayne, IN

I'm always looking for something easy to take to the lake. When it's too hot to grill, we'd much rather be relaxing in the water!

1 lb. hot dogs
2 15-oz. cans chili with beans
1 onion, finely chopped

1 t. chili powder
1 c. shredded Cheddar cheese
8 hot dog rolls, split

Place hot dogs in a slow cooker. In a bowl, combine chili, onion and chili powder; stir well and pour over hot dogs. Cover and cook on low setting for 4 to 6 hours, or on high setting for 1-1/2 to 2 hours. Add cheese just before serving; allow to melt slightly. Serve each hot dog in a roll with some chili spooned over top. Serves 6 to 8.

Grandma's Slow-Cooked Baked Beans

Tina Hengen
Clarkston, WA

Whenever I traveled to visit my grandmother, she would always have something hot and delicious ready to serve. This was one of my most favorites...it's scrumptious!

1 lb. dried navy beans
3-1/2 c. water
1 onion, chopped
4 slices bacon, chopped
1/4 c. molasses

2 t. dry mustard
1/4 t. pepper
1/8 t. ground cloves
salt to taste

In a large saucepan, cover beans with water. Bring to a boil over high heat; boil for 2 minutes. Cover pan and let stand for one hour. Drain and rinse beans; transfer to a slow cooker. Stir in 3-1/2 cups fresh water and remaining ingredients except salt. Cover and cook on low setting for 10 to 12 hours. Season with salt. Serves 10 to 12.

Georgia Green Beans & Potatoes

Tina Wright
Atlanta, GA

My aunt always said there was nothing better than a mess of fresh green beans! They're a meal in themselves with a pan of cornbread.

6 slices bacon, cut into 1-inch
    pieces and partially cooked
4 to 6 redskin potatoes, thinly
    sliced
4 to 5 c. green beans, trimmed

10-3/4 oz. can cream of celery
    soup
2 T. dried, minced onion
salt and pepper to taste

Combine all ingredients in a large slow cooker; stir gently. Cover and cook on low setting for 7 to 9 hours. Serves 4 to 6.

The best kind of friend is the kind you can sit on a porch swing with,
never say a word, then walk away feeling like it was the best
conversation you've ever had.

– Arnold Glasow

Simmered Kielbasa & Cabbage Soup

Angeline Haverstock
La Porte, IN

We go camping in Brown County in central Indiana every fall.
We put this soup in the slow cooker before we start sightseeing
for the day. It really hits the spot when we return!

1/2 head cabbage, chopped
2 potatoes, peeled and diced
2 carrots, peeled and diced
1 onion, chopped
Optional: 2 to 4 cloves garlic,
  minced

1/2 lb. Kielbasa sausage, diced
1 T. red wine vinegar
3 T. fresh dill, finely chopped
1 bay leaf
salt and pepper to taste
6 c. beef or chicken broth

Layer all ingredients in a slow cooker in order listed. Cover and cook on low setting for 5 to 6 hours. At serving time, stir well; discard bay leaf. Makes 4 to 6 servings.

Favorite stovetop soup recipes are easily converted for slow-cooking. If the soup usually simmers for 1-1/2 to 2 hours, just add all the ingredients to the slow cooker and cook on low for 6 to 8 hours. Enjoy your day of hiking, fishing or beachcombing...dinner will be ready when you get back!

All-Day Vegetable Soup

Jennie Gist
Gooseberry Patch

There's a wonderful farmers' market on the way to our favorite campsite. We always stop to pick out the veggies for this soup.

2 T. olive oil, divided
1 onion, chopped
4 cloves garlic, minced
2 to 3 carrots, diced
2 russet potatoes, peeled
    and cubed
1 turnip, peeled and diced
2 stalks celery, chopped

1/4 head cabbage, chopped
2 c. fresh green beans, trimmed
    and cut in 1-inch pieces
1/2 t. dried thyme
salt and pepper to taste
2 15-oz. cans diced tomatoes
6 c. vegetable or chicken broth

Heat one tablespoon olive oil in a large soup pot over medium-high heat. Add onion; cook until nearly translucent. Add garlic; sauté another minute, until golden. Add remaining vegetables except tomatoes; cook and stir for one to 2 minutes, adding remaining oil as needed. Stir in seasonings. Spoon mixture into a large slow cooker. Stir in tomatoes with juice and broth. Cook on low setting for 7 to 9 hours, or on high setting for 4 to 6 hours. At serving time, gently mash some of the potatoes against the side of the slow cooker to thicken the soup. Stir and serve. Makes 10 to 12 servings.

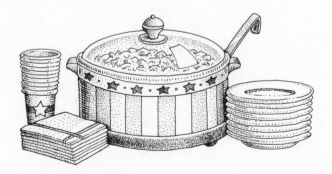

Jazz up hot soup with savory croutons! Heat one tablespoon olive oil in a large skillet. Add a big spoonful of chopped thyme, oregano and tarragon as desired, then stir in two slices of bread, cubed. Cook until lightly golden, then garnish soup servings.

Chicken Booyah

Sharon Leach
Two Rivers, WI

In northern Wisconsin, there's an annual celebration called the Community Soup. The delicious soup is simmered in huge kettles over an open fire. Everyone brings their own bowls and crackers. This is my own easy version of the soup.

1 lb. chicken, cooked and
    shredded
3 14-1/2 oz. cans chicken broth
3 potatoes, peeled and diced
1 c. fresh or frozen peas
1 c. fresh or frozen carrots,
    peeled and sliced
1 c. fresh or frozen green
    beans, sliced

1 c. fresh or frozen corn
1/2 c. celery, sliced
1/3 c. onion, chopped
2 cloves garlic, pressed
1 T. dried parsley
1/4 t. pepper
Optional: 1/2 c. water
saltines or oyster crackers

Combine all ingredients except water and crackers in a 5-quart slow cooker. Cover and cook on low setting for 5 to 6 hours, or on high setting for 3 to 4 hours. If a thinner consistency is desired, stir in water. Serve with crackers. Makes 6 to 8 servings.

Pull out your oversize coffee mugs when serving soups, stews and chili 'round the campfire. They're just right for sharing hearty servings, and the handles make them so easy to hold onto.

Beef & Barley Soup

Lisa Ann Panzino-DiNunzio
Vineland, NJ

There's nothing better than to toss some ingredients into a slow cooker, head out to your day's fun or errands and then come back to find dinner waiting for you. Serve with crusty whole-grain bread for a really satisfying meal.

1 lb. lean stew beef cubes
14-1/2 oz. can diced tomatoes
1/2 c. onion, chopped
2 stalks celery, sliced
2 carrots, peeled and sliced
3 cloves garlic, finely minced

1 c. pearled barley, uncooked
1 t. dried basil
4 c. reduced-sodium beef or
   chicken broth
sea salt and pepper to taste

Place beef, tomatoes with juice and remaining ingredients in a large slow cooker. Stir gently. Cover and cook on low setting for 6 to 8 hours. Makes 4 to 6 servings.

Take a hike while dinner simmers...bring along some trail mix
for munching. Toss together peanuts, raisins, sunflower kernels
and fish-shaped crackers and fill some little zipping bags...
a lifesaver for growling tummies!

Ruth's Champion Chili

Ruth Kaup
Springfield, MO

I won a chili cook-off with a milder version of this chili. For our church's latest cook-off, I knew I had to turn up the heat for the judges. I won! One lady shared that she had eaten two bowls full. The longer it cooks, the hotter it will become. A tablespoon of sour cream added to a bowlful will tame the heat, if preferred.

3 lbs. lean ground beef
2 onions, finely diced
2 stalks celery, finely diced
2 green peppers, finely diced
2 28-oz. cans diced tomatoes
2 40-oz. cans kidney beans,
    drained and rinsed
2 c. beef broth
10-oz. bottle steak sauce
6 T. chili powder

2 T. red pepper flakes
2 T. ground cumin
1 T. dried parsley
1 T. Worcestershire sauce
4 t. brown sugar
1 t. garlic powder
1 t. salt
6-oz. jar chopped jalapeño
    peppers
1 t. pepper

Brown beef, onions, celery and green peppers in a large skillet over medium-high heat. Drain; transfer to a large slow cooker. Add tomatoes with juice and remaining ingredients except jalapeños and pepper. Cover and cook on low setting for 5 hours. Add jalapeños and pepper; cover and cook for 2 more hours. Makes 12 servings.

Crockery Baked Potatoes

Lori Roggenbuck
Ubly, MI

Nothing beats a baked potato, and this is so easy to do!

6 russet potatoes
2 T. olive oil

1/4 t. salt
1/4 t. pepper

Pierce potatoes with a fork. Combine oil, salt and pepper in a bowl. Roll each potato in oil mixture until completely coated. Place in a slow cooker. Cover and cook for 6 hours on low setting, or for 3 to 4 hours on high setting, until tender. Serves 6.

New Mexico Green Chile Stew

*Kary Ross
Searcy, AR*

My mother created this recipe when my two sisters and I were young girls. It was a favorite of ours...anytime we could eat fresh green chiles we were all happy. Muy bueno!

3 to 3-1/2 lb. beef arm or
    chuck roast, trimmed and
    cut into chunks
1 c. beef broth
28-oz. can whole tomatoes
1 to 2 t. cumin seed
1/2 t. ground cumin

1 t. chili powder
1 t. garlic salt or powder
1 t. salt
1 t. pepper
2 bay leaves
7-oz. can diced fire-roasted
    green chiles, or to taste

Place roast in a large slow cooker. Add broth, tomatoes with juice, seasonings and enough water to fill slow cooker 2/3 full. Cover and cook on high setting for 2-1/2 hours. Remove roast to a cutting board, reserving mixture in slow cooker. Cut roast into bite-size pieces and return to slow cooker. Stir in chiles. Cover and continue to cook for an additional 1-1/2 hours. Discard bay leaves. Serves 8 to 10.

Host a chili cook-off! Ask neighbors to bring a pot of their "secret recipe" chili to share, then have a friendly judging for the best. You can even hand out wooden spoons, oven mitts and aprons as prizes!

Baja Fish Tacos

Lynda McCormick
Burkburnett, TX

Serve these tacos with black beans on the side and you have the perfect quick & easy meal! Use half green and half red cabbage, if you like.

2 c. cabbage, shredded
3 T. lime juice, divided
2 t. olive oil
1/3 c. fresh cilantro, chopped
    and divided
1 t. chili powder
1-1/4 lbs. mahi-mahi fillets,
    3/4-inch thick

8 8-inch corn tortillas, warmed
1 avocado, halved, pitted and
    thinly sliced
1/4 c. radishes, sliced
Garnish: sour cream, salsa

In a bowl, toss cabbage with one tablespoon lime juice; set aside. In a shallow dish, mix oil, remaining lime juice, one tablespoon cilantro and chili powder. Add fish to oil mixture, turning to coat all sides. Let stand for 10 minutes. Spray a countertop grill or stovetop grill pan with non-stick vegetable spray; preheat grill. Add fish and cook for 5 to 7 minutes, turning once, just until cooked through. Remove fish to a plate; break into chunks. Fill each tortilla with cabbage, fish, avocado, radishes and remaining cilantro. Top with sour cream and salsa. Makes 8 servings.

Whip up a speedy black bean salad to serve with Baja Fish Tacos.
Combine one cup drained and rinsed black beans, 1/2 cup corn,
1/2 cup salsa and 1/4 teaspoon cumin or chili powder. Chill until
serving time...easy and tasty!

Smoked Turkey-Mushroom Panini

Denise Webb
Savannah, GA

I really enjoy panini sandwiches, so after trying an especially good one in a cute little cafe, I came home and tried to duplicate it. I think mine is even better than the one I had at the cafe...oh yum!

2 slices Vienna, Italian or
   rye bread
mayonnaise or Dijon mustard
   to taste
2 slices deli smoked turkey

1 slice provolone cheese
1 to 2 T. sliced mushrooms
2 to 3 T. fresh baby spinach
2 t. butter, softened

Spread one side of each bread slice with a small amount of mayonnaise or mustard. On one bread slice, layer turkey, cheese, mushrooms and spinach; top with second bread slice. Spread outside of sandwich lightly with butter. Place sandwich on a grill pan over medium-high heat; set a heavy pan or small skillet on top to weigh down the sandwich. Cook until golden; turn sandwich and repeat on the other side. Makes one serving.

In the mood for a cookout, but it's too rainy or cold outdoors? A stovetop grill pan, countertop grill or oven broiler allow you to bring the cookout indoors. Many recipes intended for a gas or charcoal grill can be prepared using one of these options, so give it a try!

Grilled Flank Steak Sandwich

Valerie Gardner
Lyman, SC

I've been making these hearty sandwiches for years, grilling the steak in the backyard and then finishing the sandwiches indoors. On a hot summer's evening, it's nice to keep the kitchen cool!

1 to 1-1/2 lb. beef flank steak
seasoned salt and pepper
   to taste
1 sweet onion, thinly sliced
Optional: 1 green or red pepper,
   thinly sliced

2 to 3 t. olive oil
mayonnaise to taste
1 loaf sliced bread
4 to 6 slices provolone cheese
softened butter to taste

On a gas or charcoal grill, cook steak to desired doneness; add seasonings. Let steak rest for about 10 minutes; slice thinly on the diagonal. In a skillet over medium-high heat, sauté onion and pepper, if desired, in oil until caramelized. Spread mayonnaise on one side of bread. Assemble sandwiches with bread, sliced steak, onion mixture and cheese. Spread outside of sandwiches with a little butter. Heat a countertop grill, panini press or grill pan. Grill until toasted and cheese is melted. Serves 4 to 6.

Spectacular Sh'rooms

Amy Thomason Hunt
Traphill, NC

A delectable side for a steak dinner! Choose small or medium-size mushrooms for the best results.

1 lb. whole mushrooms,
   trimmed
1/4 c. canola oil
1/4 c. water

1-oz. pkg. ranch salad dressing
   mix
1 T. balsamic vinegar
1/8 t. pepper

Place mushrooms in a one-gallon plastic zipping bag. In a small bowl, combine remaining ingredients. Blend well and pour over mushrooms; seal bag and shake to coat. Refrigerate for 30 minutes, turning occasionally. Drain; arrange mushrooms on a broiler pan. Broil for 8 to 10 minutes, until tender and golden. Serves 4 to 6.

Easy Smothered Chicken

Lisa Johnson
Trenton, FL

*I came up with this dish for work one day and it was
a hit...really scrumptious!*

4 boneless, skinless chicken
   breasts
1 c. zesty Italian salad dressing

8 slices smoked bacon
4 slices Colby cheese, or
   1 c. shredded Colby cheese

Pound chicken with a meat mallet until slightly flattened. Place chicken in a large plastic zipping bag; cover with salad dressing. Seal bag and refrigerate for 2 to 4 hours. Remove chicken from bag, discarding dressing. Wrap 2 slices of bacon around each chicken piece. Spray a countertop grill with non-stick vegetable spray. Place chicken on preheated grill. Cook for about 5 to 10 minutes, until bacon is crisp and chicken juices run clear. Remove chicken to a baking pan; top with cheese. Bake, uncovered, at 350 degrees for 3 to 5 minutes, until cheese is melted. Makes 4 servings.

Serve up a salad topped with grilled apple slices...yummy with pears too!
Heat a tablespoon each of olive oil and maple syrup in a grill pan. Add thin
slices of tart apple. Cook for 6 to 8 minutes, turning once,
until deep golden and crisp. Serve warm.

Beef Gyros

Emily Mills
Pocatello, ID

You may also use thinly sliced uncooked chicken or lamb in this recipe. Mix the ingredients as with the ground beef, but sauté instead of broil. From my house to yours, enjoy!

1-1/4 lbs. ground beef
1/2 to 1 t. dried oregano
1/2 t. dried mint
1 t. salt

1 t. pepper
6 to 8 pita rounds, split
2 tomatoes, chopped

In a large bowl, mix beef and seasonings; form into 6 to 8 patties. Place patties on a broiler pan. Broil to desired doneness on both sides, about 6 inches from broiler. Serve patties in pita rounds, topped with tomatoes and Cucumber Sauce. Serves 6 to 8.

Cucumber Sauce:

3/4 c. plain yogurt
1/2 c. cucumber, chopped
1 green onion, chopped

1/2 t. dill weed
1/4 t. dried mint

In a small bowl, mix together all ingredients. Cover and refrigerate at least one hour.

Pack dips and sauces in little lidded Mason jars to take along to picnics and cookouts...easy to tuck in a cooler.

Barbecued Pork Chops

Marcia Shaffer
Conneaut Lake, PA

*It takes just a few simple ingredients to whip up
the savory marinade for these pork chops.*

8 pork chops
1/2 c. honey
1/3 c. soy sauce

2/3 c. hot water
garlic powder to taste

Arrange chops in a shallow glass dish. In a small bowl, stir together remaining ingredients; pour over chops. Cover and refrigerate overnight for 2 to 8 hours. Drain, discarding marinade. Arrange chops on a broiler pan and broil for about 10 minutes per side. Chops may also be grilled over charcoal. Makes 8 servings.

Give a lucky couple a picnic basket as a wedding gift. Filled with napkins, plates, flatware, glasses and gourmet goodies, a bow tied to the handle is all that's needed to top it off. They're sure to love it!

Broiled Honey Chicken

JoAnn
Gooseberry Patch

Delicious with coleslaw and sweet potatoes on the side. Chicken thighs are extra flavorful, but use breasts if you prefer.

4 to 6 boneless, skinless chicken thighs
1/3 c. honey
3 T. Dijon mustard

1 T. orange juice
2 t. soy sauce
1 clove garlic, minced
1/2 t. pepper

Arrange chicken on a broiler pan lined with non-stick aluminum foil. In a bowl, whisk together remaining ingredients until smooth. Brush honey mixture over chicken. Place broiler pan about 6 inches from broiler. Broil until chicken is lightly golden, about 15 minutes, basting once or twice with honey mixture. Turn chicken over; baste again. Broil another 10 minutes, or until chicken juices run clear when pierced. Chicken may also be placed in a lightly greased 13"x9" baking pan. Cover and bake at 350 degrees for 20 minutes. Turn over; baste. Cover and bake another 20 minutes, or until done. Makes 4 to 6 servings.

Share the garden's bounty when getting together for dinner with family & friends. Vintage fruit baskets found at a country flea market, lined with a tea towel or bandanna, are ideal for passing along prized tomatoes.

Flounder Clancy

Joan White
Malvern, PA

Wanting to eat more fish? It's easy with this tasty recipe.

1 lb. flounder fillets
1 sweet onion, thinly sliced and
  separated into rings

1/2 c. mayonnaise
3 T. grated Parmesan cheese
1 t. Dijon mustard

Place fish in a broiler pan lined with lightly greased aluminum foil. Arrange onion rings over fish. Combine remaining ingredients in a small bowl; mix well and spread over onion. Cover lightly with foil. Broil for 15 to 20 minutes. Uncover; broil for several more minutes, until topping is bubbly and golden. Makes 4 servings.

Herbed Broiled Tomatoes

Judy Lange
Imperial, PA

A delicious, fresh side...you can whip this up in no time!

2 tomatoes, halved
1/4 c. mayonnaise
4 t. grated Parmesan cheese

2 t. fresh dill, minced
2 t. fresh parsley, minced
salt and pepper to taste

Arrange tomatoes on a broiler pan, cut-side up. Sprinkle with salt and pepper. Mix mayonnaise, cheese and herbs in a small bowl. Spread mayonnaise mixture over tomatoes. Broil for 2 to 3 minutes, until hot and golden. Makes 4 servings.

Make clean-up easier when using the broiler...add a little water to the pan beneath the broiling rack.

Toasty Tomato-Cheese Bread

Irene Robinson
Cincinnati, OH

A different spin on French bread!

8-oz. pkg. cream cheese, cubed
1/4 c. shredded Parmesan
   cheese
1 clove garlic, pressed
2 T. fresh basil, chopped

1/4 t. salt
1/8 t. pepper
1 loaf French bread, sliced
   lengthwise
2 roma tomatoes, sliced

In a microwave-safe bowl, heat cream cheese on high for 20 seconds. Stir in Parmesan cheese, garlic and seasonings. Place bread on a broiler pan, cut-side up. Spread cream cheese mixture over cut sides of bread. Top with tomato slices. Broil for 4 to 5 minutes, until bubbly and golden. Slice to serve. Serves 6 to 8.

Heirloom tomatoes are showing up everywhere. What sets them apart from more modern tomatoes is that the seeds have been handed down from one family member to another for many generations. Give them a try and pick up a basket the next time you see them!

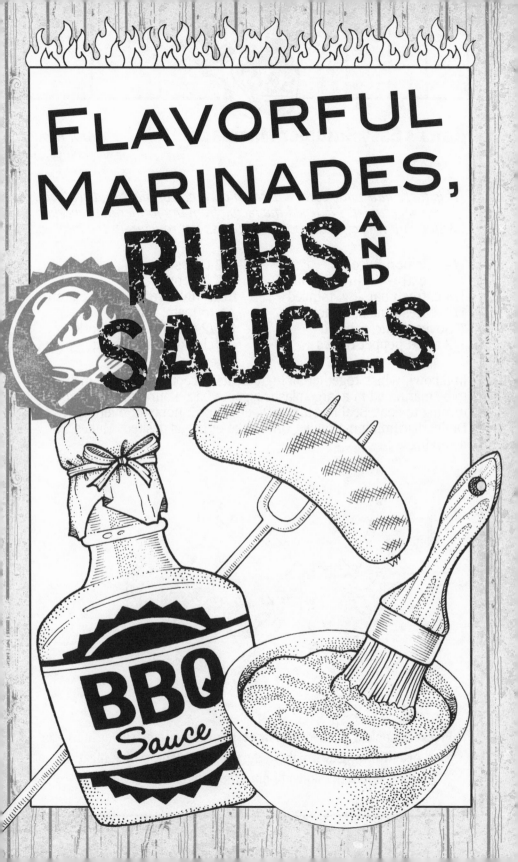

FLAVORFUL MARINADES, RUBS AND SAUCES

BBQ Sauce

Anna's Easy Summer Marinade

Ann Brown
Niles, MI

This tasty marinade can be used on all kinds of meat and seafood... even vegetables. I learned the recipe from my former housekeeper Anna. She was a great cook, and I miss her touches in the kitchen.

1/4 c. lemon juice
1/2 c. extra-virgin olive oil
1/4 c. fresh parsley, minced
1/4 c. fresh basil, minced
3 cloves garlic, minced
1/2 t. red pepper flakes

1/2 t. kosher salt
1/2 t. pepper
fresh dill, oregano and cilantro
   to taste, minced
1-1/2 to 2 lbs. beef, pork,
   chicken or seafood

In a bowl, whisk together all ingredients except meat. Place meat to be marinated in a large plastic zipping bag. Pour marinade over top, turning to coat. Seal bag and refrigerate for 2 hours or overnight. Drain, discarding marinade. Grill, bake or fry as desired. Makes 4 servings.

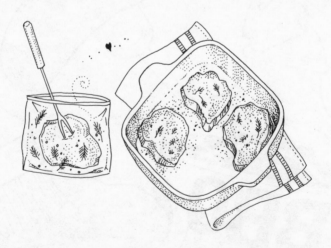

Freeze uncooked chicken, beef or pork cutlets with marinade in freezer bags. After thawing overnight in the fridge or picnic cooler, meat can go right into the skillet or onto the grill for a savory meal.

Grilled Chicken Marinade

Mitchell Snay
Columbus, OH

*When the weather is nice, we like to grill dinner outdoors
instead of using the stovetop, so we're always looking
for good chicken marinades. This one is delicious!*

1/4 c. lemon juice
2 T. olive oil
2 cloves garlic, minced
1/2 t. dried oregano

1/2 t. dry mustard
salt to taste
1-1/2 to 2 lbs. boneless, skinless
   chicken breasts

Mix together marinade ingredients. Flatten chicken slightly and place
in a shallow glass dish. Pour marinade over chicken, turning to coat
well. Cover and refrigerate for 2 to 8 hours. Drain, discarding
marinade. Grill chicken as desired. Serves 4 to 6.

Pork Chop Marinade for Grilling

Judy Larson
Hastings, MI

*Delicious marinated pork chops are a holiday favorite of ours.
Great for pork tenderloin too.*

4 thick pork chops, butterflied
3 T. soy sauce
1 T. brown sugar, packed

2 cloves garlic, minced
1 t. ground coriander
1 t. pepper

Place pork chops in a large plastic zipping bag. Stir together marinade
ingredients in a bowl; pour over pork chops. Seal bag and refrigerate
for 2 to 4 hours. Drain, discarding marinade. Grill chops for 5 minutes
per side, until juices no long run pink. Serves 4.

Mix up some chili salt to sprinkle on hot
buttered corn! Just combine 4 teaspoons
chili powder with 2 teaspoons kosher
salt in a shaker.

Hunk o' Steak Pineapple Marinade

Anne Girucky
Norfolk, VA

My sister Robin gave me this recipe back in the early 1980s, and I've enjoyed it ever since. It makes a mouthwatering London broil. After being marinated for 2 days, the flavor is truly wonderful.

2 c. olive oil
1 onion, chopped
1/2 c. red steak sauce
1/2 c. Worcestershire sauce
20-oz. can pineapple chunks
2 c. regular or non-alcoholic beer

1 c. white wine or beef broth
2 T. granulated garlic
1 T. seasoned salt
3 to 4 lbs. beef flank steak

In a large saucepan over medium heat, combine olive oil, onion and sauces. Cook, stirring occasionally, for 5 to 10 minutes. Add pineapple with juice and remaining ingredients except steak. Simmer an additional 5 to 10 minutes; let cool. Pour marinade with pineapple over steak in a shallow glass dish. Cover and refrigerate for 8 hours to 2 days, turning steak occasionally. Drain, discarding marinade. Place pineapple chunks on skewers. Grill steak and pineapple skewers to desired doneness. To serve, slice steak thinly on the diagonal. Serves 6 to 8.

Revive the drive-in movie tradition in your own backyard! Call a local camera or rental store for a video projector...simply hook it to a DVD player and project your favorite movie on a big white sheet or painter's cloth. Sure to be a hit!

Karen's Soy Beef Marinade

Gladys Kielar
Whitehouse, OH

My neighbor Karen just moved away this past January. I will remember her fondly for sharing this recipe over 20 years ago. It is good on any kind of beef...it softens the meat and makes it so juicy and tender. I love it especially for steaks. You'll love it too!

3/4 c. oil	1 clove garlic, minced,
1/4 c. soy sauce	or 1/4 t. garlic salt
3 T. honey or sugar	Optional: 1 green onion,
2 T. cider vinegar or lemon juice	chopped
1/2 t. ground ginger	2 lbs. beef steak

Whisk together marinade ingredients. Pour over steak in a large plastic zipping bag. Seal bag and refrigerate for 4 to 5 hours, turning occasionally. Drain, discarding marinade. Grill steak as desired. Makes 4 to 6 servings.

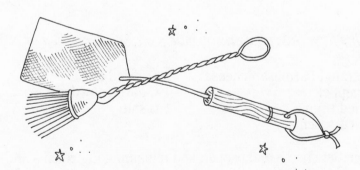

For the most mouthwatering marinated chops and steaks, pat the meat dry with a paper towel after draining off the marinade. Then sprinkle on any seasonings before placing it on the hot grill.

Roy's Steak Seasoning

Linda Rich
Bean Station, TN

One day I was surprised to find that our favorite steak seasoning was no longer being made. I experimented and created this seasoning mix. My husband said he couldn't tell the difference! It's delicious on just about anything, even beef stew. We've given jars of it to friends for Christmas gifts. They love it and hint often for refills!

1 c. dried, minced onion
4 c. kosher salt
1 c. coarse pepper

1 c. granulated garlic
1 c. paprika

In a food processor, finely chop onion to same consistency as other ingredients. Combine all ingredients in a bowl; mix well. Store in airtight containers. To use, sprinkle to taste over steak, burgers, chicken and pork loin while grilling. For a smaller quantity, measure with tablespoons instead of cups. Makes 7 cups.

Mediterranean Herb Rub

Tori Willis
Champaign, IL

This flavorful rub works wonders on grilled chicken or beef.

1/3 c. grated Parmesan cheese
1/3 c. pepper
2 T. dried thyme
2 T. dried rosemary

2 T. dried basil
1 t. garlic powder
1 t. salt

Mix together cheese and pepper; add remaining ingredients and stir well. If a finer texture is desired, process in a food processor. Store in an airtight container up to one week. To use, rub over chicken or beef; grill as desired. Makes one cup.

A vintage wooden soft-drink crate
makes a handy picnic carrier.

All-Purpose Barbecue Rub

Sandy Dayhoff
Hanover, PA

A friend shared a tasty barbecue rub with me. When I ran out of it and checked the price, I decided to make my own! It's excellent on beef and pork, even fish and chicken.

1/4 c. brown sugar, packed
1 T. chili powder
1 T. paprika
1 T. kosher salt
2 t. garlic powder
2 t. onion powder

1 t. ground celery seed
1 t. ground cumin
1 t. dried oregano
1 t. pepper
1/2 t. cayenne pepper

Mix together all ingredients; place in a shaker container with a lid. To use, sprinkle generously on chicken, pork or beef or fish before grilling, baking or slow cooking. Makes about 2/3 cup.

Secret BBQ Dry Rub

Sherry Carrier
Kenduskeag, ME

My family's best grilling secret for delicious pork ribs...beef too!

1/2 c. brown sugar, packed
1 T. chili powder
1 T. salt
1 t. onion powder
1 t. garlic powder
1/2 t. cayenne pepper

1/2 t. seafood seasoning
1/2 t. dried thyme
2 to 3 lbs. southern-style
   pork ribs
favorite barbecue sauce
   to taste

Mix together brown sugar and seasonings; store in a covered container. To use, rub over both sides of ribs. Let stand at least 10 minutes, or cover and refrigerate up to 6 hours. Grill ribs, basting with barbecue sauce as desired. Makes 4 servings.

Barb's Teriyaki Sauce

Barb Rudyk
Alberta, Canada

This sauce is sweet, not salty or strong-tasting like some teriyaki sauces. You'll love it in your favorite teriyaki chicken recipe. It is very good with cooked rice too.

1/2 c. light or regular soy sauce	1 T. cornstarch
3/4 to 1 c. brown sugar, packed	1/4 t. garlic powder
3/4 c. water	1/8 t. ground ginger

Combine all ingredients in a saucepan; whisk to mix well. Bring to a boil over medium-high heat, stirring constantly, until mixture boils and thickens slightly. Cool to room temperature. To use, brush over chicken when grilling or baking. Makes 1-1/2 cups sauce.

Pack some favorite seasonings or sauces into a barbecue gift bag for a much-appreciated hostess surprise! Cut two back pockets from a pair of old blue jeans, arrange on the front of a white gift bag and secure with hot glue. Slip a sassy red bandanna in one pocket and a few recipe cards in the other.

Tangy Apple BBQ Sauce

Jonathan Bastian
Mifflinburg, PA

*I created this sauce to complement steak on the grill. It is
the perfect addition to grilled burgers...great for pulled pork too.*

1 c. catsup
1/2 c. brown sugar, packed
1/4 c. honey
1/4 c. molasses
1/4 c. Worcestershire sauce
1/2 t. pepper

1/4 t. smoke-flavored cooking
  sauce
1/8 t. chili powder
1 apple, peeled, cored and finely
  diced

Combine all ingredients in a saucepan over medium heat. Simmer,
stirring occasionally, until thickened. Serve with grilled burgers or
steak. Makes 2 cups.

Bar-B-Que Burger Sauce

Paulette Downton
Franklin, IN

*This sauce turns an ordinary hamburger into an extraordinary one.
It is delicious...just try it and see for yourself!*

1/4 c. catsup
3 T. brown sugar, packed

1 t. dry mustard
1/4 t. nutmeg

Combine all ingredients; mix well. To use, brush sauce over one side
of burgers; place on grill sauce-side down. Grill as desired, brushing
additional sauce over other side of burgers. Makes 5 servings.

A tray of warm, moistened towels is a
must when serving sticky barbecue ribs!
Dampen fingertip towels in water and
a dash of lemon juice, roll up and
microwave on high for 10 to 15 seconds.

Savory Shish-Kabob Sauce

Sonya Smith
Roxboro, NC

*I love the orange flavor of this sauce, so I always measure
the orange juice by heaping spoonfuls. For a spicier sauce,
add more red pepper flakes.*

1/2 c. brown sugar, packed
2 T. frozen orange juice
   concentrate

2 T. teriyaki sauce
2 T. water
1/8 t. red pepper flakes

Mix all ingredients in a small saucepan over medium heat. Bring to
a boil; reduce heat to low. Simmer for 5 minutes, stirring often.
Remove from heat; pour a small amount into a cup. To use, brush
sauce from cup over shish-kabobs during last few minutes of grilling.
Arrange grilled kabobs on a bed of cooked rice in a serving platter.
Spoon remaining sauce from saucepan over kabobs and rice. Makes
4 servings.

Need a super-quick marinade? Grab a bottle of Italian salad dressing...
it's terrific with just about any kind of meat. Add 1/4 to 1/2 cup marinade
per one to two pounds of meat. You only need enough to coat, not cover!

Microwave Texas BBQ Sauce

Faith Deaton
Southaven, MS

This sauce is delicious with Texas-style BBQ beef brisket. When my husband and I first married, we moved to Texas where beef is king. I was given this recipe by my husband's cousin...it's been a family favorite ever since!

2 T. butter
1 onion, finely chopped
2 T. green pepper, minced
1 clove garlic, pressed
3/4 c. catsup

1/4 c. cider vinegar
1/4 c. dark brown sugar, packed
1/4 t. dry mustard
1/8 t. hot pepper sauce

Combine butter, onion, green pepper and garlic in a microwave-safe casserole dish. Microwave, uncovered, on medium-low for 2 to 3 minutes. Stir in remaining ingredients. Cover and microwave on 3/4 power for 2-minute intervals until mixture is bubbly. Serve sauce with barbecue beef brisket. Makes 8 to 12 servings.

For a quick and casual centerpiece, curl a string of dried chile peppers into a circle, then set a hurricane with a fat red candle in the center.

Dad's Savory Steak Butter

Cathy Gearheart
Narrows, VA

My dad couldn't stand what he called "dry meat." This flavorful butter adds just the right tang to pork chops and beef steaks.

1/2 c. butter, softened
2 T. red steak sauce
1 T. Worcestershire sauce
1 t. smoke-flavored cooking
   sauce

1/8 t. hot pepper sauce
1 clove garlic, pressed
1/2 t. seasoned salt
6 pork rib chops, 1-inch thick
pepper to taste

In a small bowl, beat together butter, sauces, garlic and salt. Cover and refrigerate for at least 30 minutes to allow flavors to blend. To use, season pork chops with pepper. Grill over medium heat until just done, about 12 to 15 minutes. Serve pork chops dolloped with steak butter. Makes 6 servings.

Gorgonzola Steak Butter

Marion Sundberg
Ramona, CA

A yummy topping for any grilled beef steak!

1/3 c. butter, softened
1/2 c. crumbled Gorgonzola
   cheese
2 T. balsamic vinegar

2 cloves garlic, minced
1 t. dried basil
pepper to taste

Mix all ingredients until well blended. To use, add a dollop of steak butter to steak just before removing from grill. Serves 6 to 8.

To poke a wood fire is more solid enjoyment
than almost anything else in the world.

– Charles Dudley Warner

Flavorful Marinades, Rubs & Sauces

Chimichurri Sauce

Jen Thomas
Santa Rosa, CA

When I first tried this traditional green herb sauce from Argentina, I knew I had to learn to make it myself! It's a delicious way to use fresh herbs from the farmers' market.

1-1/2 c. fresh flat-leaf parsley, packed
3/4 c. extra-virgin olive oil
3 T. white wine vinegar
2 T. fresh oregano, chopped
6 cloves garlic, quartered
1/4 t. red pepper flakes
salt and pepper to taste

Combine all ingredients in a food processor; process until smooth. May be refrigerated up to 4 hours. Bring to room temperature; serve with grilled beef, chicken or fish. Makes 4 servings.

Fresh Cali Salsa

Judith Cozatt May
Woodhaven, MI

I'm from California and I love Mexican food. I like to serve this spicy salsa on California beef tri-tip. We use it on just about anything...even omelets!

6 roma tomatoes, chopped
2 bunches fresh cilantro, coarsely chopped
1 red onion, chopped
3 jalapeño peppers, diced
juice of 1 lime
1/8 t. coarse salt

Combine all ingredients in a bowl; toss to mix well. Cover and refrigerate for several hours to combine flavors. Serves 4.

Pamela's Tartar Sauce

Pamela Bennett
Whittier, CA

When I was a young adult, fish was a very scary food! My husband and kids really liked frozen fish sticks. I did too, but something just seemed to be missing. I played with various tartar sauce recipes and came up with this one! Now I serve many types of fresh fish for dinner. For the zingiest flavor, use fresh-squeezed lemon juice.

1 c. mayonnaise
3 T. sweet pickle relish
3 T. onion, finely chopped

3 T. catsup
3 T. lemon juice
2 t. dill weed

In a small container with a lid, mix all ingredients well. Cover and refrigerate up to one week. Serve with fish. Makes 4 to 6 servings.

Lemon-Garlic Grilling Sauce

Cheryl Panning
Wabash, IN

Be prepared to share this recipe whenever you serve it...
you will be asked for it!

1/4 c. lemon juice
1/4 c. butter, melted
1/4 c. olive oil

1 T. green hot pepper sauce
3 cloves garlic, minced

Combine all ingredients; blend well. To use, brush on fish, seafood, chicken or vegetables while grilling. Bring any remaining sauce to a full boil; serve with grilled food. Makes 3/4 cup.

Pack up your fishing gear and head to a peaceful lake or shady riverbank.
Even if you don't catch any fish, you'll enjoy a day of relaxing fun!

Cucumber Dill Sauce

Susan Shilo
Rochester, NY

When I was growing up, my mom always fixed cucumbers & cream as a cool, refreshing summer side dish. This is a version of that dish to use as a condiment. It's especially tasty spooned over salmon, tilapia, shrimp and steak...even grilled vegetables.

1 cucumber, peeled and divided
8-oz. container sour cream
1 T. fresh dill, chopped,
    or 1 t. dill weed

zest and juice of 1 lemon
1 t. sugar
salt and pepper to taste

Grate 1/4 of the cucumber into a bowl; set aside. Dice remaining cucumber into 1/2-inch cubes and add to grated cucumber. Stir in remaining ingredients; mix thoroughly. Cover and chill until ready to serve, about 30 minutes. Makes 10 to 12 servings.

Crisp coleslaw pairs well with grilled fish. Perk up your favorite coleslaw with some mandarin oranges or pineapple tidbits for a delicious change.

Barbecued Onion Relish

Charmie Fisher
Fontana, CA

This recipe came from my mother-in-law. She shared it with me at one of our family barbecues, and I've kept it ever since. It's so yummy on everything grilled! I especially like it on grilled sausages.

3 T. canola oil
4 onions, halved and sliced
1 T. sugar
1/2 t. salt
4 cloves garlic, chopped
1 T. chili powder
1/4 t. red pepper flakes

1/2 c. hickory-flavored barbecue sauce
1/2 c. beer or chicken broth
1 T. molasses
1 T. Dijon mustard
1 T. red wine vinegar
2-1/2 t. soy sauce

Heat oil in a large saucepan over medium heat. Add onions; sprinkle with sugar and salt. Cover and cook, stirring occasionally, until onions are soft and juicy, but not browned, about 30 minutes. Add garlic, chili powder and red pepper flakes. Sauté for 4 minutes. Stir in remaining ingredients; reduce heat. Simmer, uncovered, stirring occasionally, until mixture thickens slightly, about 10 minutes. Cool to room temperature. Cover tightly and refrigerate for 24 hours to allow flavors to develop. May be made up to one week ahead. To serve warm, simmer over low heat. Makes 8 servings.

A bundle of fresh-cut herbs makes such a fragrant cook-out centerpiece!
Bunch together sprigs of dill, rosemary, mint, basil or thyme
in an old-fashioned canning jar and tie with jute.

Special Hamburger Sauce

Barb Rudyk
Alberta, Canada

It turns an ordinary burger into a favorite fast-food version.

1 c. mayonnaise
1/3 c. creamy French salad
  dressing
1/4 c. sweet pickle relish

1 T. sugar
1 t. dried, minced onion
salt and pepper to taste

Combine all ingredients in a bowl; stir well. Cover and refrigerate up to one week. Serve over grilled burgers. Makes 12 servings.

Olive Burger Topping

Mary Hall
Kentwood, MI

Remember the olive burgers back in the 1950s? Just add a sesame bun, sliced tomato and lettuce for a mouthwatering treat!

8-oz. pkg. cream cheese,
  softened
1 c. sliced green olives with
  pimentos

6 T. olive juice
1/2 onion, finely chopped
Optional: chopped green chiles
  to taste

Mix together all ingredients, stirring well to blend in olive juice. Cover and chill at least 2 hours. Serve on grilled burgers as desired. Makes 6 to 10 servings.

Pick up a stack of vintage plastic burger baskets. Lined with crisp paper napkins, they're still such fun for serving burgers and fries... clean-up after dinner is a snap too!

Grandma's Fresh Relish

Kathleen Whitsett
Greenwood, IN

When my grandma was a small girl in the 1920s, she and her father befriended a little old street vendor. He made this wonderful fresh relish for the hot dogs that he sold out of his street-corner cart. The vendor liked my grandma so much that he gave his relish recipe to her father. When I was growing up, Grandma would let me make this relish with her. Those wonderful memories will never be forgotten.

1 cucumber, peeled and diced
3 green onions, diced, both
    white and green parts
1 green pepper, diced

1 tomato, diced
1-1/2 T. sugar
salt and pepper to taste

Combine all ingredients in a bowl; stir well. Cover and chill. The vegetables will create a wonderful juice. Serve with hot dogs or brats, or as a chilled salsa with chips. Makes 6 to 8 servings.

Hot Dawg Sauce

Pam Massey
Marshall, AR

This sauce is worthy of your favorite grilled Polish hot dog and the best hot dog roll you can find! It's so simple to share good food and fond memories made around the campfire or fire pit.

3/4 c. catsup
3/4 c. brown sugar, packed
1/4 c. honey

1 t. cider vinegar
1 t. soy sauce
1/2 t. onion powder

Combine all ingredients in a saucepan over medium heat. Cook and stir just to boiling. Drizzle over grilled hot dogs. Serves 8 to 10.

ICY-COLD FRESH SALADS

Parmesan Caesar Potato Salad

Wendy Reaume
Chatham, Ontario

When I was young, my family owned a food company that made cold salads for supermarkets and restaurants. Potato salad was one of their specialties. Grandpa sold the company in the mid-1980s, yet his recipes are still enjoyed in our family. I love that history! But I just wasn't a fan of potato salad until I tried it Caesar-style. The creamy, tangy flavor is a real crowd-pleaser!

4 lbs. new potatoes, boiled
    and quartered
6 slices bacon, crisply cooked
    and crumbled

1/2 bunch green onions,
    chopped
Garnish: shredded Parmesan
    cheese

While potatoes are still warm, combine with bacon and onions in a large bowl. Add Light Caesar Dressing; toss gently to mix. Top with Parmesan cheese. Serve immediately, or cover and chill; flavor will be even better the next day. Makes 8 to 10 servings.

Light Caesar Dressing:

1 c. light mayonnaise
3 T. red wine vinegar
1/3 to 1/2 c. shredded Parmesan
    cheese
3 cloves garlic

2 t. Worcestershire sauce
1 to 1-1/4 t. Dijon mustard
1/2 t. dry mustard
pepper to taste
1/4 c. olive oil

Add all ingredients except olive oil to a food processor. Process until well combined. With food processor still running, slowly pour in oil until well blended.

Keep salads chilled...simply nestle
the salad serving bowl into a larger
bowl filled with ice cubes.

172

Tomato & Sweet Corn Salad

Lois Wetton
Temple City, CA

My camping group enjoys this refreshing salad when we're on the road. I've had this recipe for many years and make it with fresh vegetables from my garden whenever I can.

6 ears yellow or white corn, husked
1-1/2 lbs. roma tomatoes, diced
3/4 c. red onion, chopped
1/2 c. fresh cilantro, chopped
1/4 c. extra-virgin olive oil
1 T. red wine vinegar
salt and pepper to taste

Bring a large pot of water to a boil over high heat. Add corn; cook for 5 minutes. Drain; cool to room temperature. Cut kernels from cobs and place in a large bowl. Add tomatoes, onion, cilantro, oil and vinegar. Toss lightly until well blended. Season with salt and pepper. Serve immediately, or cover and chill for one hour to overnight. Serves 6 to 8.

Snippy Snappy Coleslaw

Brenda Melancon
McComb, MS

I serve this colorful coleslaw often when we cook out. We also take this dish along to picnics with our friends.

1/4 c. mayonnaise
1/4 c. sweet pickle relish
2 T. ranch salad dressing
2 T. sugar
1 T. white wine vinegar
1/2 t. dry mustard
1/2 t. paprika
1/4 t. dill weed
16-oz. pkg. 3-color shredded coleslaw mix

In a large bowl, combine all ingredients except coleslaw mix. Whisk until smooth. Add coleslaw mix; stir until well combined. Cover and chill at least one hour before serving. Makes 4 to 6 servings.

Loy's Vegetable Salad

*Loy Nicley
Washburn, TN*

*I make this salad often in the summertime for homecomings
and Memorial Day celebrations. Everyone always
asks my wife if I've brought my salad...they love it!*

3 roma tomatoes, chopped
3 pickling cucumbers, chopped
1 red onion, chopped
1 green pepper, chopped

1 red pepper, chopped
1 yellow pepper, chopped
8-oz. bottle Italian salad
   dressing

Combine all vegetables in a large bowl. Pour enough dressing over
vegetables to cover. Stir gently to mix. Cover and refrigerate for several
hours to overnight. Makes 12 servings.

Enjoy a special lunch just for two. On a sunny day, pack a bicycle
basket with a cozy fleece blanket, wrapped sandwiches and
a thermos of lemonade, then take a bike ride in the country
with a special friend!

Sicilian Cucumber Salad

Cynde Sonnier
La Porte, TX

I brought this light and refreshing salad to a barbecue cookout, and it was a big hit! It goes especially well with grilled hamburgers.

4 cucumbers, sliced
1 red onion, sliced
1 red pepper, sliced
10 green olives with pimentos,
    sliced

4 t. extra-virgin olive oil
1-1/2 t. white wine vinegar
1 t. sugar
salt and pepper to taste

Combine all vegetables in a large bowl; set aside. In a small bowl, whisk together olive oil, vinegar and sugar. Add to cucumber mixture and toss well. Season with salt and pepper. Serve immediately, or cover and chill. Serves 6.

For a convenient and fun way to serve picnic salads, spoon individual portions into wide-mouth mini Mason jars. Secure the lids, and when it's serving time, friends will find the tasty salad, and its dressing, stays right inside the jars!

Paulette's Potato Salad

Paulette Downton
Franklin, IN

Over the years I've tried several potato salad recipes, but I keep coming back to this one. It's tried & true.

1 c. mayonnaise
2 T. white vinegar
1 t. sugar
1-1/2 t. salt
1/4 t. pepper
1 c. celery, sliced

1/2 c. onion, chopped
4 c. redskin potatoes, peeled, cubed and cooked
2 eggs, hard-boiled, peeled and chopped

In a large bowl, stir together mayonnaise, vinegar, sugar and seasonings. Add remaining ingredients; toss to coat well. Cover and chill for 2 hours before serving. Makes 6 servings.

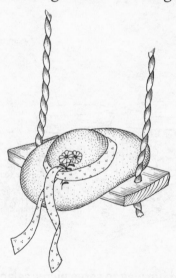

The camp hummed with voices. There was the shrill shouting of children, merry-mouthed as young guinea hens, the scraping of deck chairs, the creak-squeak of swings. A calling of greetings, "Well, if it isn't Cousin Bessie! When did you get in?"

– Clementine Paddleford

Marinated Green Bean Salad

Marion Satterthwaite
Blairstown, NJ

The first time I made this salad for a family gathering, it was a huge hit. It is now requested for every occasion. Enjoy the dish and the compliments you'll receive!

2 lbs. green beans, trimmed
1/2 c. red onion, chopped
1/4 c. olive oil
1/4 c. cider vinegar

2 T. sugar
3/4 t. salt
Garnish: coarsely chopped
  fresh dill

Cover beans with salted water in a large saucepan. Bring to a boil over medium-high heat. Reduce heat to low. Cover and simmer for about 10 minutes. Drain well; let beans cool and place in a large bowl. Whisk together remaining ingredients in a small bowl; pour over beans. Cover and chill at least one hour to overnight to allow beans to absorb dressing. Garnish with dill. Serves 6.

Sandra's Tomatoes & Chives

Kelli LeRiche
New Boston, MI

We used to have cookouts quite often at my parents' home, and they would invite our neighbor Sandra to come over. This dish that she brought was the simplest and the tastiest too!

4 to 6 ripe tomatoes, sliced
1 cucumber, peeled and sliced

cider vinegar to taste
Garnish: snipped fresh chives

Arrange tomato and cucumber slices in a circular pattern on a serving plate. Drizzle with vinegar; sprinkle with chives. Serve immediately. Makes 4 to 6 servings.

Crisp Spinach Salad

Cathy Barr
Logansport, IN

We love this salad with grilled steak or pasta dishes.

2 bunches fresh spinach, torn
  and stems removed
2 cucumbers, peeled and diced
1 c. celery, sliced
1/2 c. pine nuts

1/2 c. black olives, quartered
1/2 c. green olives with
  pimentos, quartered
1/2 c. fresh flat-leaf parsley,
  minced

Combine all ingredients in a large bowl. Drizzle with Olive Oil Dressing; toss to mix well. Makes 6 to 8 servings.

Olive Oil Dressing:

3/4 c. olive oil
1/4 c. red wine vinegar
1/8 t. dried oregano

1 t. salt
pepper to taste

Whisk or shake together all ingredients.

Garnish cool garden salads with warm grilled pita wedges for
a delicious contrast. Simply place pita rounds directly on a
hot grill until toasty. Cut into wedges.

Bacon-Ranch Deviled Eggs

Andrea Heyart
Aubrey, TX

My mother-in-law used to make deviled eggs with ranch dressing.
Over the years, I've added my own little touches to her recipe.
This version is my favorite!

1 doz. eggs, hard-boiled
   and peeled
1/4 c. mayonnaise
1 to 2 T. ranch salad dressing
1 t. horseradish sauce

4 slices bacon, crisply cooked
   and crumbled
Optional: snipped fresh chives,
   grated Parmesan cheese

Slice eggs in half lengthwise; place yolks in a bowl. Mash yolks with
a fork; mix in mayonnaise, salad dressing, horseradish and bacon.
Spoon yolk mixture into each egg white half; arrange on a platter.
Garnish with chives and Parmesan cheese as desired. For the best
flavor, cover and chill for at least 30 minutes before serving. Makes
2 dozen.

Toting deviled eggs to a carry-in? Nestle the eggs in a bed of
curly parsley or shredded lettuce to keep them from sliding
around...they'll arrive looking as scrumptious as they taste!

Zesty Marinated Garden Veggies

Hazel Powell
McLeansville, NC

I catered a family reunion with pork barbecue, grilled chicken and all the usual sides on the menu. I had just picked veggies from the garden, so I thought, "How about giving them a taste of something new?" Everyone raved about it and wanted the recipe!

1 c. cucumber, sliced
1 c. yellow squash, sliced
1 c. zucchini, sliced
1 c. tomato, quartered
1/2 c. broccoli flowerets
1/2 c. cauliflower flowerets
1/2 c. red onion, sliced
1/2 c. green pepper, sliced
1/2 c. celery, sliced
8-oz. bottle zesty Italian
  dressing
1 t. salt-free herb seasoning

Combine all vegetables in a large bowl. Add salad dressing and seasoning; toss to mix. Cover and refrigerate for 2 hours before serving. Makes 10 to 12 servings.

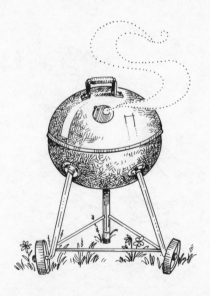

Backyard cookouts aren't just for summertime...fall is a terrific time to gather friends and family and enjoy the crisp air. Play touch football, jump into a pile of leaves, tell ghost stories...be a kid again!

Rosy Beet & Potato Salad

Janis Parr
Ontario, Canada

Beets and potatoes may seem like an unusual combination, but this dish is a very old country favorite that has been enjoyed at many church socials and potlucks. It tastes yummy and looks gorgeous with the ruby-red color of the beets.

8 to 10 redskin potatoes, peeled
    and boiled
1-1/2 c. mayonnaise, divided
1 c. canned pickled beets,
    drained and 1/2 c. juice
    reserved

1/2 c. onion, minced
salt and pepper to taste
Optional: lettuce leaves

In a large bowl, mash potatoes while still warm. Add one cup mayonnaise and stir well to combine. Add beets and reserved beet juice; mash into potatoes. Stir in onion, salt and pepper. Line a large bowl with lettuce leaves, if desired. Spoon salad into bowl. Spoon remaining mayonnaise over top of salad. Cover and chill for 2 hours before serving. Makes 8 servings.

Toting a salad to a get-together? Mix it up in a plastic zipping bag, seal and set it on ice in a picnic cooler. When you arrive, pour out the salad into a bowl. No more worries about leaks or spills!

Zippy Tomato-Cauliflower Toss
Yvonne Van Brimmer
Apple Valley, CA

This is my yummy way to get my kids to eat fresh veggies.
They love it with any kind of barbecued meat!

2 beefsteak tomatoes, cubed
2 c. cauliflower flowerets
1 red onion, sliced and separated
   into rings

2 t. Salad Herb Seasoning
salt to taste
1 c. zesty Italian salad dressing

Combine all vegetables in a large bowl. Sprinkle with Salad Herb Seasoning and salt. Drizzle with salad dressing and toss to mix. Cover and chill for one hour to overnight. Serves 4 to 6.

Salad Herb Seasoning:

2 t. sesame seed
1 t. dried oregano
1 t. dried basil
1 t. dried rosemary

1 t. dried thyme
1 t. granulated garlic
1 t. salt
1/2 t. sugar

Combine all ingredients in a small jar and shake. Keep covered.

Did you buy a bunch of fresh herbs for a recipe that calls for just a couple of tablespoons? Chop the extra herbs and toss them into a lettuce salad! Fresh dill, parsley, thyme, chives and basil all add a delightful punch of flavor.

Fresh Watermelon Salad

Angie Biggin
Lyons, IL

You'd never guess that this cool, light and refreshing summer salad is low-fat! It complements grilled chicken and fish perfectly.

6 to 8 c. Boston bibb lettuce, torn
1 English cucumber, halved and thinly sliced
1/2 c. red onion, very thinly sliced

2 c. seedless watermelon cubes
1/2 c. raspberry vinaigrette salad dressing
1 T. olive oil mayonnaise
1 t. poppy seed

Combine lettuce, cucumber, onion and watermelon in a large bowl; set aside. In a small bowl, whisk salad dressing gradually into mayonnaise until well blended. Add to salad; toss gently to coat. Sprinkle with poppy seed just before serving. Serves 6 to 8.

Cucumber-Tomato Salad

Elizabeth Breese
Naperville, IL

I learned this recipe from Mom, and she served it all summer long using fresh veggies grown in Dad's garden. Almost any flavor of salad dressing works, so there are lots of possibilities!

1 to 2 cucumbers, peeled and sliced
2 to 3 tomatoes, sliced into thin wedges

1/2 onion, thinly sliced
8-oz. bottle Italian or ranch salad dressing

Combine all vegetables in a bowl. Add desired amount of salad dressing; mix well. Serve immediately, or cover and chill. Serves 4 to 6.

Let the kids invite a special friend or two home on a cookout night. Keep it simple with grilled burgers and a crisp salad. A great way to get to know your children's playmates!

Ranch Cornbread Salad

Ruby Pruitt
Nashville, IN

*I like taking different dishes to our church pitch-in dinners,
and this one was a big hit! With its layered colors, this hearty
salad looks very pretty in the clear glass bowl I use.*

8-1/2 oz. pkg. cornbread mix
1 c. mayonnaise
1 c. sour cream
1-1/2 T. ranch salad dressing
  mix
16-oz. can pinto beans, drained
1/4 c. sweet onion, chopped

2 tomatoes, chopped
1 green, yellow or red pepper,
  chopped
16-oz. can corn, drained
1 lb. bacon, crisply cooked and
  crumbled
2 c. shredded Cheddar cheese

Prepare and bake cornbread mix according to package directions; let
cool. Meanwhile, in a small bowl, mix together mayonnaise, sour
cream and salad dressing mix; cover and refrigerate. Crumble cooled
cornbread into a deep clear glass bowl. Layer with beans, onion,
tomatoes, pepper, corn and bacon. Spread mayonnaise mixture over
top; sprinkle with cheese. Serve immediately, or cover and chill until
serving time. Makes 10 servings.

Kitchen tea towels are a must for drying just-rinsed garden vegetables.
They're reusable too...much less wasteful than paper towels! Dress up
plain cotton towels in a jiffy by stitching on bands of vintage fabric.

Zesty Fiesta Corn Salad

Brenda White
Bluff City, TN

This salad is good tasting and quick to prepare. Perfect for warm days, yet easy to make and serve year 'round.

1/4 c. water	15-oz. can corn, drained
2 T. taco seasoning mix	1/2 c. black olives
1/4 c. oil	1/4 c. red pepper, diced
1 T. vinegar	1-1/2 c. tomatoes, diced

In a bowl, stir together water and taco seasoning; whisk in oil and vinegar. Add remaining ingredients and toss lightly to coat. Cover and refrigerate for several hours to overnight before serving. May be kept refrigerated up to 3 days. Makes 8 servings.

For hearty salads in a snap, keep unopened cans of diced tomatoes, olives, garbanzo beans and marinated artichokes in the fridge. They'll be chilled and ready to toss with fresh greens or cooked pasta at a moment's notice.

Blue Cheese Slaw

Melissa Knight
Athens, AL

What's a cookout without the perfect coleslaw? Here is a scrumptious and easy twist on typical slaw recipes.

2 c. green cabbage, shredded
2 c. red cabbage, shredded
2 c. carrots, peeled and shredded
3/4 c. mayonnaise
1 T. Dijon mustard
1-1/2 t. dry mustard

1-1/2 t. seasoning salt
1-1/2 t. cider vinegar
salt and pepper to taste
3/4 c. crumbled blue cheese
2 T. fresh parsley, minced

In a large bowl, combine cabbage and carrots. In a smaller bowl, combine remaining ingredients except cheese and parsley. Pour mixture over cabbage; toss well to coat. Stir in cheese and parsley. Cover and refrigerate for at least 2 hours before serving. Makes 10 to 12 servings.

Serve up a salad buffet for a warm-weather get-together! Try a grilled chicken salad, a pasta salad, a crisp green tossed salad and a fruity gelatin salad. Crusty bread and a simple dessert complete a tasty, light meal.

Fire & Ice Tomatoes

Michelle Marberry
Valley, AL

*Don't be fooled...this icy-cold salad is not spicy at all! It's perfect
for potlucks or served over lettuce leaves at a luncheon.*

5 tomatoes, cut into wedges
1 white onion, sliced and
   separated into rings
3/4 c. white vinegar
1/4 c. water

6 T. sugar
1 T. mustard seed
1/4 t. cayenne pepper
1 cucumber, peeled and sliced

Combine tomatoes and onion in a large bowl; set aside. In a small
saucepan, combine vinegar, water, sugar and spices. Bring to a boil
and cook for one minute, stirring until sugar dissolves. Pour over
tomatoes and onion; gently toss to coat. Cover and refrigerate for at
least 2 hours. Add cucumber; toss to coat. Refrigerate 8 hours to
overnight before serving. Makes 8 servings.

Iceberg lettuce is best pulled apart by hand, not cut with a knife. Try this
old trick for coring a head easily. Hold the lettuce with the bottom side
facing the kitchen counter. Bring it down hard on the counter...
the core will loosen and can be pulled right out.

Antipasto on a Stick

Lisa Terlesky
Canfield, OH

*Everybody loves finger food! These yummy kabobs are
so quick & easy for get-togethers anytime.*

10 8-inch skewers
20 green olives with pimentos
20 thin slices hard salami
20 cubes mozzarella or
   provolone cheese

20 thin slices pepperoni
20 cheese-stuffed tortellini,
   cooked
20 black olives

Thread all ingredients onto skewers in the order listed, folding salami
and pepperoni slices into quarters as you go. Makes 10 servings.

Pineapple-Carrot Coleslaw

Arlene Smulski
Lyons, IL

*Crisp coleslaw gets a sweet and crunchy punch with
carrots and pineapple. I can't get enough of it!*

3 c. cabbage, shredded
8-oz. can unsweetened crushed
   pineapple, drained
3/4 c. carrot, peeled and
   shredded

1/3 c. mayonnaise
1 T. sugar
1 T. white vinegar

Mix together cabbage, pineapple and carrot in a bowl. In a small bowl,
whisk together remaining ingredients. Pour over cabbage mixture; toss
to coat. Cover and chill for 2 to 3 hours before serving. Makes 4 to
6 servings.

Fill up a big party tray with crisp
  veggies for dipping...calorie-
counting friends will thank you!

Seasonal Fruit Bowl

Susan Kruspe
Hall, NY

*So refreshing on a warm summer day! Other fruits
may be added, depending on what's in season.*

2 c. water
1-1/2 c. sugar
3 T. lime juice
1 seedless watermelon, halved
    and cubed
1 cantaloupe, halved, seeds
    removed and cubed

6 plums, halved, pitted and
    sliced
4 nectarines, halved, pitted and
    sliced
1 lb. seedless green grapes

In a saucepan over medium heat, combine water, sugar and lime juice.
Cook, stirring often, for about 15 minutes, until mixture becomes
syrupy. Cover and refrigerate until well chilled. Place fruit in a large
bowl; pour chilled syrup over fruit. Cover and refrigerate at least
one hour to allow flavors to blend, stirring occasionally. Makes 12 to
16 servings.

Always a summer favorite...a watermelon half, filled with melon balls,
blueberries, strawberries, sliced peaches and other fresh fruit. Toss with
a little lemon juice and honey for a tempting treat.

Confetti Corn Salad

Jamie Kehres
Delaware, OH

This salad goes very well with grilled steaks...
terrific for cookouts and picnics. Enjoy!

2 c. corn	2 T. olive oil
1 c. tomato, diced	1 t. lime juice
1/4 c. red pepper, diced	1/4 t. ground cumin
1/4 c. green pepper, diced	1/4 t. salt
2 T. red onion, diced	1/4 t. pepper
1 T. fresh cilantro, chopped	

Combine all vegetables and cilantro in a bowl; set aside. Whisk together remaining ingredients in a small bowl; pour over vegetable mixture and toss to mix well. Serve immediately, or cover and chill until serving time. Serves 4 to 6.

Snip some blossoms from the market-fresh bouquet on your table to garnish a fresh salad...there are lots of edible flowers to enjoy. Pesticide-free blooms like pansies, violets, calendulas, lilacs and nasturtiums are just a few you'll find delicious.

Jalapeño Potato Salad

Sarah Woodruff
Austin, TX

My dad has always loved this yummy potato salad with a festive kick...it's really delicious with barbecue. When I made it for my stepfather's company potluck, everyone was amazed at how tasty it was. I was thrilled!

6 redskin potatoes, peeled, cubed and cooked
2 eggs, hard-boiled, peeled and chopped
2 stalks celery, chopped
2 jalapeño peppers, seeded and chopped

1/4 c. onion, chopped
1/4 c. mayonnaise
3 T. spicy brown mustard
1/4 t. ground cumin
1/4 t. pepper
Optional: 1/8 t. hot pepper sauce

In a large bowl, combine potatoes, eggs, celery, jalapeños and onion; set aside. In a small bowl, combine remaining ingredients; mix well. Pour mayonnaise mixture over potato mixture; toss gently to coat. Cover and refrigerate overnight. Makes 6 to 8 servings.

Save a step by boiling eggs and potatoes at the same time! Cook the potatoes in a large pot of boiling water for about 10 minutes. Add the eggs to the pot and cook for another 15 minutes. Remove from heat; drain.

Edna's Refrigerator Pickles

Marsha Houston
Crossville, TN

These tasty bread & butter pickles keep very well. This recipe is from my wonderful friend and neighbor Ms. Edna, who would have been happy that I've shared it with Gooseberry Patch. She lived to her mid-90s and is remembered warmly by all who knew her.

1 c. pickling cucumbers,
    thinly sliced
Optional: 1 green pepper,
    thinly sliced
1 c. onion, thinly sliced

1 c. white vinegar
2 c. sugar
1 t. pickling salt
1 t. mustard seed
1 t. celery seed

In a gallon jar or a large glass container with a cover, mix together cucumbers, green pepper and onion. Combine remaining ingredients; mix well (no cooking is necessary). Pour vinegar mixture over cucumber mixture. Let stand at room temperature for 2 hours. Cover and refrigerate for 5 days before serving to allow flavors to blend. Keep refrigerated up to one month. Makes one quart.

Here's an idea for easy, quick pickled eggs...just add peeled, hard-boiled eggs to a jar of pickled beets. Store in the fridge for a few days. The eggs will absorb the beet juice...a great addition to your relish tray!

DELICIOUS DESSERTS AND REFRESHING BEVERAGES

Grilled Pineapple Sundaes

Cheri Maxwell
Gulf Breeze, FL

Luscious! Grilling really transforms slices of juicy ripe pineapple.

1/2 c. brown sugar, packed
2 T. butter, melted
2 T. lemon juice
1 t. cinnamon
1 pineapple, peeled, cored and
    sliced 1-inch thick

Garnish: vanilla ice cream
Optional: toasted coconut,
    maraschino cherries

In a bowl, mix brown sugar, butter, lemon juice and cinnamon. Brush mixture over both sides of pineapple slices. Grill pineapple over high heat for about one minute on each side, until golden. Remove each slice to a dessert plate. Serve warm, topped with a scoop of ice cream and garnished as desired. Serves 4 to 6.

As the sun goes down, lanterns filled with citronella oil are a must...
they'll light your campsite with a warm glow and repel pesky
mosquitoes too. At home, hang lanterns on your porch or
deck to create a cozy atmosphere.

Dutch Oven Peach Cobbler

Cheryl Panning
Wabash, IN

I've been making this dessert since I was a new bride over 40 years ago. It's very easy to do and the results are delicious!

29-oz. can sliced peaches,
    drained
1-1/2 c. sugar, divided
1 t. butter, melted
1 c. all-purpose flour

2 t. baking powder
1/2 t. salt
1/2 c. milk
1/2 c. water

Prepare a campfire with plenty of hot charcoal briquets. Place peaches in a greased 10" Dutch oven; set near fire to warm. In a bowl, mix 1/2 cup sugar and butter. In a separate bowl, mix flour, baking powder and salt. Stir flour mixture and milk into sugar mixture. Pour batter over peaches. Sprinkle with remaining sugar; pour water over batter without stirring. Arrange 7 hot charcoal briquets in a ring; set Dutch oven on top. Add lid; place 14 briquets on lid. Cook for about one hour, until bubbly and golden. Every 15 minutes, carefully rotate Dutch oven 1/4 turn to the right and rotate lid 1/4 turn to the left. Replace briquets on lid as needed. Cobbler may also be baked in a greased 10" round baking pan. Bake at 350 degrees for one hour. Serve warm. Makes 6 to 8 servings.

After dessert, take everyone on a nature hike at a nearby park or around the neighborhood. Take along a pocket-size nature guide, a magnifying glass and a tote bag to bring back special finds. Fun for young and old, and a great way to lose that too-full feeling!

Pie Iron Apple Pies

Karen Burger
Clear Spring, MD

It's impossible to count the number of things you learn in Girl Scouts. My parents took my troop camping often and we made pie-iron everything! Enjoy your pie by the campfire that cooked it.

2 slices bread
1 T. butter, softened
3 T. canned apple pie filling

3 T. apple, peeled, cored
   and diced
cinnamon to taste

Spread one side of each bread slice with butter. Place one bread slice butter-side down in a pie iron. Spread with pie filling. Top with apple, cinnamon and remaining bread slice, butter-side up. Close pie iron; cook over campfire for about 5 minutes per side, until toasted and golden. Makes one serving.

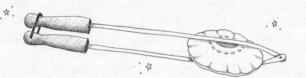

Chuck Wagon Cherry Pies

Annette Ingram
Grand Rapids, MI

My favorite campfire treat! When I was growing up, I never wanted to wait long enough for my pie to cool, but it's worth the wait.

1 baked pound cake, sliced
   1/2-inch thick
4 to 5 T. butter, softened

Optional: 1 t. almond extract
21-oz. can cherry pie filling
Garnish: powdered sugar

Spread one side of each cake slice lightly with butter. Stir extract, if using, into pie filling. For each pie, place one slice of cake butter-side down in a pie iron; top with one to 2 tablespoons pie filling and a second slice of cake, butter-side up. Close pie iron. Cook over campfire until hot and toasted, 4 to 6 minutes per side. Sprinkle with powdered sugar. Makes 8 servings.

Yummy Banana Boats

Jen Licon-Connor
Gooseberry Patch

We like to make these on our family camping trips, and our daughters both love them. Once my oldest daughter asked if she could have another one...but without the banana this time!

4 bananas
1/2 c. semi-sweet chocolate
   chips

1/2 c. mini marshmallows
Optional: 1/2 c. chopped peanuts

For each banana, pull back one section of peel without removing it; cut out a wedge lengthwise in the banana. Fill with chocolate chips, marshmallows and peanuts, if using. Pat peel back into place; wrap banana in aluminum foil. Cook bananas in campfire coals or on a hot grill for 5 minutes, or until chocolate and marshmallows are melted. Bananas may also be baked at 350 degrees for 7 to 10 minutes. Let cool slightly before unwrapping. Makes 4 servings.

A basket of pine cone fire starters is a special gift! Carefully melt old candle ends in a double boiler and use tongs to dip pine cones. Sprinkle with a little glitter if you like, then set on wax paper to dry.

Grilled Peaches

Lisa Ann Panzino-DiNunzio
Vineland, NJ

A unique way to serve up one of summer's sweet natural delights!

4 peaches, halved and pitted
2 T. butter, melted

cinnamon to taste
8 scoops vanilla ice cream

Brush the cut side of each peach half lightly with butter. Place peaches cut-side down on a hot grill. Reduce heat and grill for 8-10 minutes, until tender. Remove to serving bowls. Sprinkle with cinnamon. Top with a scoop of ice cream. Serves 8.

Grilled Camp Bananas

Shannon Reents
Loudonville, OH

A few years ago, our boys were going to camp, and my husband and I were asked to be the camp cooks all week. When we agreed, we didn't know we would not have a stove! Everything was to be cooked on an open fire. I had a few months to prepare recipes and a grocery list. It all turned out great! We've been asked to return every year. This is one of my recipes...the kids love it!

6 firm bananas
2 T. brown sugar, packed

1/4 t. cinnamon

Place unpeeled bananas on campfire, 4 to 6 inches from medium-hot coals. Cook for 10 to 12 minutes, turning once, until peels are brown and bananas are soft. Combine brown sugar and cinnamon in a cup. Split peels lengthwise; sprinkle bananas with brown sugar mixture. Serves 6.

Packing for a camping trip? Be sure to bring a big bag of marshmallows for toasting...everyone in camp will come running!

Roasted Apple & Ice Cream

Janice Bonner
Ontario, Canada

One of my favorite things to make around the fire pit.
It's delish...even better topped with homemade ice cream!

1 baking apple, cored
cinnamon to taste

1 scoop vanilla ice cream

Wrap apple in aluminum foil; place on hot coals in campfire or fire pit. Cook for 15 to 20 minutes. Remove from coals; unwrap apple carefully and place in a dessert bowl. Sprinkle with cinnamon and top with a dollop of ice cream. Serves one.

A roomy galvanized washtub makes a clever ice chest. Fill it up with ice, juice boxes, bottles of water or soda, and they'll stay frosty all day long. Perfect for chilling watermelons too!

Apple Pie Sundaes

Janis Greene
Brandon, FL

This fun recipe is easily increased for a larger group.

3 to 4 Granny Apples, peeled,
   cored and chopped
1/4 c. sugar
1/4 c. water
3/4 t. cinnamon

1/4 t. nutmeg
Garnish: crushed shortbread
   cookies, vanilla ice cream
Optional: whipped cream

In a saucepan over medium heat, combine apples, sugar, water and spices. Bring mixture to a boil. Reduce heat to medium-low; cover and simmer for 10 minutes, until apples are tender. Remove from heat and let cool. To serve, layer apple mixture with cookie crumbs and ice cream in individual parfait glasses or a serving dish. Top with whipped cream, if desired. Makes 4 servings.

If ants are such busy workers, how come
they find time to go to all the picnics?
— Marie Dressler

Chocolate Burritos

Joni Wallman
Indianapolis, IN

A great recipe that can be made ahead for camping trips. Yummy with a scoop of ice cream and drizzled with chocolate sauce!

1 flour tortilla	1 to 2 T. chocolate chips
1 to 2 T. peanut butter	1 to 2 T. mini marshmallows

Place tortilla on a piece of aluminum foil. Spread with a thin layer of peanut butter; sprinkle with chocolate chips and marshmallows. Fold in the end of the flour tortilla and roll up. Wrap folded tortilla in foil. Cook over a campfire or grill until ingredients are melted, or bake at 350 degrees for 10 to 12 minutes. Serves one.

Grilled Peanut Butter S'Mores

Rebekah Tank
Mount Calvary, WI

Even better than regular s'mores...give them a try, I bet you'll agree! You can use any kind of chips too, peanut butter, milk chocolate, butterscotch or mix it up. Yummy!

8 frozen waffles, any variety	1 c. mini marshmallows
1 c. peanut butter chips	

Place 4 waffles on separate squares of greased aluminum foil. Top with peanut butter chips, marshmallows and remaining waffles. Fold foil over waffles; wrap in another layer of foil. Grill, covered, over medium heat for 8 to 10 minutes, until chips and marshmallows are melted, turning once. Unwrap carefully. Makes 4 servings.

Fresh Fruit Tart

Amanda Bennett
Rindge, NH

I took a couple of different tart recipes and combined my favorite ingredients. I made some very festive tarts for the 4th of July, and partygoers raved about them! You can use one cup each of three favorite soft fruits...chopped kiwi fruit are good.

18-oz. tube refrigerated sugar
   cookie dough, softened
8-oz. pkg. cream cheese,
   softened
1/4 c. sugar

1/2 t. almond extract
1 c. fresh blueberries
1 c. fresh raspberries
1 c. fresh strawberries, hulled
   and halved

Press cookie dough onto an ungreased 12" round pizza pan. Bake at 350 degrees for 10 to 15 minutes, until golden. Cool on a wire rack until set. In a bowl, beat cream cheese, sugar and extract until smooth. Spread over cooled crust. Arrange berries in the center of tart in the shape of a star; add a border with more berries. Refrigerate until serving. Cut into wedges to serve. Serves 8.

It's lots of fun to go to a berry farm to pick your own sweet berries.
There's nothing like the taste of farm-fresh berries in a wonderful cake,
cobbler or pie...or simply nibbled right from the bucket! Pack up
the kids, fill up a thermos with frosty lemonade and enjoy
a memorable day together in the country.

Mud Pie

Judy Handschug
White City, OR

This chocolatey, easy-to-make "pie" was such a hit in our family that now all the adults request it for their birthdays!

1-1/2 c. chocolate wafer cookies, finely crushed
1/4 c. butter, melted
1/2 gal. mocha ice cream, softened

1 to 1-1/2 12-oz. jars hot fudge ice cream topping
Garnish: whipped cream

In a bowl, mix crushed cookies with melted butter; press into the bottom of an ungreased 8" round springform pan. Bake at 350 degrees for 10 minutes. Remove from oven; let cool on a wire rack or speed up cooling in freezer. Spoon softened ice cream into pan. Cover and freeze until ice cream is solid. Warm fudge topping according to label directions; drizzle over ice cream. Return to freezer until serving time. To serve, remove ring from pan and let stand several minutes at room temperature. Cut into wedges and top with whipped cream. Makes 8 servings.

If you're toting a dessert to a potluck or carry-in, secure the lid with a colorful tea towel wrapped around the baking dish and knotted at the top. Tuck a serving spoon inside the knot...it's at your fingertips!

Strawberry Gratin

Lisa Kastning
Marysville, WA

One of my very favorite recipes...it's delicious and so easy. I make it every strawberry season and everyone loves it!

8 c. strawberries, hulled
   and quartered
1-1/2 c. sour cream
2 T. half-and-half

1/8 t. salt
1/2 c. dark brown sugar, packed
Optional: ice cream, pound cake

Place strawberries in an ungreased 13"x 9" baking pan. In a bowl, whisk together sour cream, half-and-half and salt. Spoon mixture evenly over berries. Sprinkle brown sugar over sour cream mixture. Broil until brown sugar has melted and is lightly golden. Serve as is, or spooned over ice cream or slices of pound cake. Serves 6.

Bring a pail so kids can collect seashells at the beach or pine cones and rocks in the woods. Set the kids down with craft glue, wiggly eyes and pipe cleaners...they can turn their "finds" into funny creatures!

Louisiana Pear Cake

Heather Nance
Danbury, TX

This recipe has been passed down for generations. I remember as a young girl going to my Aunt Faye's house at the crawfish farm in Louisiana and eating this delicious pear cake. I can still hear our laughter, sitting around the dinner table eating crawfish with fresh-baked cake for dessert.

1/2 c. butter, softened
1 c. sugar
1 egg
1-1/2 c. all-purpose flour
1 T. baking soda
1/4 t. salt

1/2 t. cinnamon
1 t. vanilla extract
2 c. pears, peeled, cored
  and grated
1/2 c. chopped pecans
Garnish: whipped cream

In a bowl, beat together butter, sugar and egg. In a separate bowl, sift together flour, baking soda, salt and cinnamon; add to sugar mixture. Add vanilla, pears and nuts; mix well. Pour batter into a greased and floured 8"x8" baking pan. Bake at 300 degrees for one hour. Serve with whipped cream. Makes 8 servings.

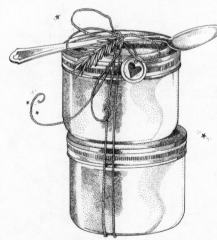

Serve up cobbler parfaits in mini Mason jars or small glasses. Alternate scoops of fruit cobbler or crisp and layers of ice cream. Garnish with whipped topping and a sprig of fresh mint. Fun for picnics and cookouts!

Jenny's Indoor S'mores

Jenny Lynch
Blue Springs, MO

One Father's Day when our first baby was just a few months old, we decided to head to the lake with my parents for a little fishing trip. My husband and my dad both have a huge sweet tooth, so I wanted to bring a dessert that would hold up in June's heat. This rich dessert tastes like s'mores, but there's no need to make a campfire!

18-oz. tube refrigerated sugar
    cookie dough, softened
12-oz. pkg. milk chocolate
    chips, divided

1/2 c. marshmallow creme
1 c. mini marshmallows
Optional: ice cream

Press cookie dough into an ungreased 8-1/2" springform cake pan. Bake at 350 degrees for about 10 minutes, until golden. Cool on a wire rack. Place half of the chocolate chips in a microwave-safe bowl. Microwave for one minute; stir until smooth and chips are melted. Spread melted chocolate over baked crust. Cover and refrigerate until chocolate hardens. Spread marshmallow creme over melted chocolate layer; sprinkle with marshmallows and remaining chocolate chips. Return to oven until marshmallows are golden, about 3 to 4 minutes. Serve warm or cold, cut into wedges and topped with ice cream, if desired. Makes 8 to 10 servings.

Who doesn't love an ice cream float on a sunny day? Set out tall glasses filled with scoops of vanilla ice cream and an assortment of fruit-flavored soda pop for guests to choose their favorite. Add some striped straws, just for fun!

Karen's Pineapple Sheet Cake

Tiffani Schulte
Wyandotte, MI

My mom started making this yummy cake back in the 1970s when Texas sheet cake first became really popular. I like this cake even better than its chocolate cousin...and that's really saying something!

18-1/2 oz. pkg. yellow or white
    cake mix
2 20-oz. cans crushed pineapple
1/4 c. cornstarch
2-1/4 c. sugar, divided

3-oz. pkg. cook & serve vanilla
    pudding mix
1 c. milk
1 c. shortening or butter
Optional: finely chopped walnuts

Prepare cake mix according to package directions; pour batter into a greased 15"x10" jelly-roll pan. Bake at 350 degrees until a toothpick tests clean, about 15 minutes. Let cool. Meanwhile, in a saucepan over medium heat, combine pineapple with juice, cornstarch and 1-1/4 cups sugar. Cook and stir until thickened. Let cool. In a separate saucepan over medium heat, combine dry pudding mix and milk. Bring to a boil; cook and stir until thickened. Let cool. In a large bowl, with an electric mixer on medium, beat together shortening or butter and remaining sugar until fluffy. Add cooled pudding to shortening mixture. Beat on high for 5 to 10 minutes, until very light and fluffy. Spread frosting over cooled cake; top with cooled pineapple mixture. Sprinkle with walnuts, if desired. Serves 12 to 18.

If you see a vintage cake pan with its own slide-on lid at a tag sale, snap it up! Not only is it indispensible for toting cakes and bar cookies to a picnic, it also makes a clever lap tray for kids to carry along crayons and coloring books on car trips.

Mom's Homemade Ice Cream

Lu Madru
Carlisle, AR

The best! This recipe is the only one my family ever used with our old hand-cranked ice cream freezer. It's written on the back of a 1950s grocery receipt. It has a delicious custard-like taste. Mom often added chopped ripe strawberries or peaches.

1 qt. whole milk
5-oz. can evaporated milk
4 eggs, beaten

1 c. sugar
1 t. vanilla extract, or more
    to taste

Mix all ingredients in a large saucepan over medium-low heat. Cook until very hot, but not quite to a boil, whisking constantly. Remove from heat and let cool. Cover and chill mixture until cold. Pour into an ice cream freezer. Freeze according to manufacturer's directions. Makes 12 servings.

Butter Pecan Ice Cream

Cyndi Little
Whitsett, NC

A special summer treat! This ice cream is a wonderful change from plain vanilla or chocolate.

1/3 c. chopped pecans
1 T. butter
1 c. brown sugar, packed
1-1/2 c. half-and-half

2 eggs, beaten
1/2 c. whipping cream
1 t. vanilla extract

In a small skillet over medium heat, sauté pecans in butter until lightly golden, stirring frequently. Set aside. In a saucepan over low heat, stir together brown sugar, half-and-half and eggs until smooth. Bring to a simmer, stirring occasionally; cook 2 minutes more. Remove from heat; stir in cream, vanilla and pecans. Pour mixture into an ice cream freezer. Freeze according to manufacturer's directions. Makes 4 servings.

Homemade Peach Ice Cream

Lori Vincent
Alpine, UT

This is my family's favorite summertime recipe! I started making it when my husband and I were first married 30 years ago. We would make a bucket of ice cream and invite friends over to play board games. It's a great way to get to know your neighbors and create some long-lasting memories.

12 to 14 ripe peaches, peeled,   2-1/2 c. sugar
    halved and pitted, or   6 T. lemon juice
    2 qts. home-canned   1 qt. half-and-half, divided
    peaches, drained   1 qt. whipping cream

Purée peaches in a blender; transfer to a large heavy saucepan. Add sugar, lemon juice and 2 cups half-and-half. Cook over low heat until sugar dissolves, stirring frequently. Remove from heat; let cool. Stir in cream and remaining half-and-half. Cover and chill mixture well, overnight if possible. Pour into an ice cream freezer. Freeze according to manufacturer's directions. Makes 4 quarts.

Just-made homemade ice cream is delicious but very soft.
For firmer, scoopable ice cream, transfer it to a plastic freezer
container and place in the freezer compartment for one hour
to overnight...if you can wait that long!

Knob Creek Lemonade

Kassie Frazier
West Point, TN

I've always loved ice-cold lemonade, and my two girls enjoy setting up their own little lemonade stand. So I was ecstatic when my mother-in-law gave me her very own best-ever lemonade recipe!

3 c. sugar
12 c. cold water, divided

6 lemons, halved
ice cubes

Add sugar and 2 cups water to a one-gallon pitcher; stir and let stand. Squeeze lemon halves into pitcher; add 4 or 5 of the lemon halves to pitcher. Add remaining water; stir until sugar is dissolved. Chill; serve over ice. Makes one gallon.

Garnish cool beverages with fruit-flavored ice cubes.
Cut favorite soft fruits like watermelon, cantaloupe, kiwi or
honeydew melon into cubes, purée in a food
processor and freeze in ice cube trays.

Pool Party Punch

Janis Parr
Ontario, Canada

This fresh and tangy punch is perfect on a hot summer's day when the girls come over for a visit.

4 c. cold water
2 c. sugar
48-oz. can orange juice
48-oz. can pineapple juice
48-oz. can grapefruit juice

1/2 c. lemon juice
4 c. ginger ale, chilled
Garnish: orange and lime slices,
  maraschino cherries

Combine water and sugar in a saucepan over medium heat. Bring to a boil; cook and stir until sugar dissolves. Remove from heat and allow to cool. Combine sugar mixture and juices in a large pitcher or punch bowl; stir to combine. Chill. Just before serving, add ginger ale; garnish as desired. Serves 10 to 12.

For simple table decorations, place round pebbles in the bottom of Mason jars and fill with water. Then tuck in bunches of sweet daisies or sunflowers and tie a bow around jar necks with jute.

Tampa Tea

Sandy Atkinson
Bloomington, IN

A flavorful change from ordinary ice tea! We like to serve this tea at cookouts. My kids love it and still ask for it when they come home.

3 tea bags
1 c. boiling water
4 c. cold water
2-1/2 c. orange juice

1/4 c. lemon juice
1/2 c. sugar
ice cubes

In a large pitcher, add tea bags to boiling water. Let stand about 5 minutes; discard tea bags. Stir in cold water, juices and sugar. Stir until sugar dissolves. Serve over ice. Serves 4 to 6.

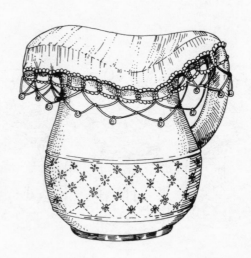

It's easy to keep pesky bugs away from frosty pitchers of
ice tea or lemonade...simply stitch buttons or charms
to the edges of tea towels and drape
over the pitchers.

Piña Colada Slush

Charlotte Smith
Tyrone, PA

A cool and refreshing beverage that's welcome any time of the year, even at holiday parties.

3 6-oz. cans pineapple juice
10-oz. can frozen non-alcoholic
   piña colada mix
2-qt. container diet or regular
   sweetened lemonade drink
   mix

2 c. cold water
1 T. lime juice
2-ltr. bottle lemon-lime soda,
   chilled

In a large bowl, combine pineapple juice, piña colada mix, lemonade drink mix, water and lime juice. Stir until drink mix is dissolved. Transfer to a plastic freezer container. Cover and freeze for 6 hours to overnight. Remove from freezer for 45 minutes before serving. For each serving, combine 1/2 cup slush mix with 1/2 cup soda in a tall glass. Makes 12 servings.

Save on bottled water and soda pop...keep a chilled pitcher of water in the fridge for a refreshing thirst quencher anytime. If your family enjoys flavored water, add a few lemon wedges, orange slices or sprigs of fresh mint.

Muddled Peach Tea

Kelly Gray
Weston, WV

A perfect gallon of peach tea! Down south, peaches are supreme for sweetness. Be sure to use real vanilla for the best flavor.

8 tea bags
2 c. boiling water, divided
2 c. sugar
4 ripe peaches, peeled, halved
    and pitted

1 t. vanilla extract
ice cubes

Add tea bags to one cup boiling water; cover and let steep for 11 minutes. Meanwhile, dissolve sugar in remaining boiling water. Purée peaches and vanilla in a blender. Stir together all ingredients in a one-gallon pitcher; serve over ice. Makes one gallon.

Set out stacks of colorful bandannas...they make
super-size fun napkins when enjoying picnic foods.

Sharon's Watermelon-Ade

Sharon Jones
Oklahoma City, OK

Perfect for picnics or just enjoying in your own backyard.
Serve in Mason jars...fun and so refreshing!

1 c. fresh mint, torn
3/4 c. plus 1 T. sugar, divided
4-3/4 c. cold water, divided
5 c. watermelon, cubed

1-1/2 c. fresh lemon juice,
  or to taste, strained
ice cubes

In a large pitcher, use a wooden spoon to crush mint with one tablespoon sugar. In a small saucepan over medium heat, combine 3/4 cup water and remaining sugar. Simmer, stirring occasionally, for abut 5 minutes, until sugar dissolves; cool. Purée watermelon in a blender; strain, reserving juice. Add watermelon juice, lemon juice and sugar mixture to pitcher with mint. Add remaining cold water; stir until combined. Chill; serve over ice. Makes 1/2 gallon.

A new terra cotta pot makes a terrific ice bucket. Simply line the pot with wax paper, fill with ice and add a new garden trowel.

Strawberry Lemonade Sipper

Laura Lane
Carthage, MO

This is one of my "do with what you've got" recipes that I just made up. The kids insisted that I write down the recipe.

1 c. frozen strawberries
2 T. lemon juice, or to taste
1 c. sugar

16-oz. bottle seltzer or soda
water, chilled
ice cubes

Place all ingredients except ice in a blender. Fill blender to the top with ice; blend until slushy. Pour into glasses. Serves 4.

Keep bugs away from your cool glasses of lemonade...
simply poke a hole through a paper cupcake liner,
add a straw, flip it upside-down and use it
as a beverage cap. So clever!

BURNING QUESTIONS...
ANSWERED!

Is it time to cook?

If you can hold your hand comfortably 5 inches over the coals:

5 to 6 seconds = low heat, or 250 to 300 degrees

4 seconds = medium heat, or 350 to 400 degrees

2 seconds = high heat, or 400 to 450 degrees

Is the meat done yet?

Use an instant-read thermometer to check for the recommended minimum internal temperature:

beef = 145 degrees (medium rare)   fish & seafood = 145 degrees

burgers = 160 degrees   pork = 145 degrees

chicken = 165 degrees

Meats continue to cook inside and rise about 10 more degrees off the fire, so they can actually be taken off at a slightly lower temperature.

Is it time to eat?

Remove grilled meats to a platter and let them rest or stand for 10 to 15 minutes before slicing and serving...they'll be nice and juicy!

INDEX

INDEX

INDEX

Find Gooseberry Patch
wherever you are!
www.gooseberrypatch.com

Call us toll-free at 1·800·854·6673

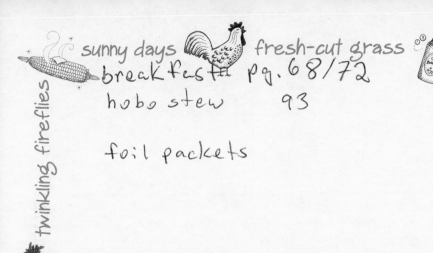

sunny days   fresh-cut grass

breakfast pg. 68/72

hobo stew   93

foil packets

twinkling fireflies

smiling sunflowers

floppy straw hats

strawberry picking

county fairs   sun-ripened tomatoes

U.S. to Metric Recipe Equivalents

Volume Measurements

1/4 teaspoon	1 mL
1/2 teaspoon	2 mL
1 teaspoon	5 mL
1 tablespoon = 3 teaspoons	15 mL
2 tablespoons = 1 fluid ounce	30 mL
1/4 cup	60 mL
1/3 cup	75 mL
1/2 cup = 4 fluid ounces	125 mL
1 cup = 8 fluid ounces	250 mL
2 cups = 1 pint =16 fluid ounces	500 mL
4 cups = 1 quart	1 L

Weights

1 ounce	30 g
4 ounces	120 g
8 ounces	225 g
16 ounces = 1 pound	450 g

Oven Temperatures

300° F	150° C
325° F	160° C
350° F	180° C
375° F	190° C
400° F	200° C
450° F	230° C

Baking Pan Sizes

Square		Loaf	
8x8x2 inches	2 L = 20x20x5 cm	9x5x3 inches	2 L = 23x13x7 cm
9x9x2 inches	2.5 L = 23x23x5 cm	Round	
Rectangular		8x1-1/2 inches	1.2 L = 20x4 cm
13x9x2 inches	3.5 L = 33x23x5 cm	9x1-1/2 inches	1.5 L = 23x4 cm